Higher
English
Practice Papers for SQA Exams

Colin Eckford

Contents

Introduction	iii
Revision grid	vi
Practice Paper A	1
Practice Paper B	33
Practice Paper C	63
Answers	93

HODDER
GIBSON
AN HACHETTE UK COMPANY

The Publishers would like to thank the following for permission to reproduce copyright material:

Exam rubrics at the start of each paper and the Critical Essay supplementary marking grid on pages 126, 160 and 192 reproduced by permission copyright © Scottish Qualifications Authority.

Acknowledgements: please refer to page 193.

Every effort has been made to trace all copyright holders, but if any have been inadvertently overlooked the Publishers will be pleased to make the necessary arrangements at the first opportunity.

Although every effort has been made to ensure that website addresses are correct at time of going to press, Hodder Gibson cannot be held responsible for the content of any website mentioned in this book. It is sometimes possible to find a relocated web page by typing in the address of the home page for a website in the URL window of your browser.

Hachette UK's policy is to use papers that are natural, renewable and recyclable products and made from wood grown in sustainable forests. The logging and manufacturing processes are expected to conform to the environmental regulations of the country of origin.

Orders: please contact Bookpoint Ltd, 130 Park Drive, Milton Park, Abingdon, Oxon OX14 4SE. Telephone: (44) 01235 827720. Fax: (44) 01235 400454. Lines are open 9.00–5.00, Monday to Saturday, with a 24-hour message answering service. Visit our website at www.hoddereducation.co.uk. Hodder Gibson can be contacted direct on: Tel: 0141 333 4650; Fax: 0141 404 8188; email: hoddergibson@hodder.co.uk

First published in 2017 by
Hodder Gibson, an imprint of Hodder Education,
An Hachette UK Company
211 St Vincent Street
Glasgow G2 5QY

Impression number   5 4 3 2 1
Year   2021 2020 2019 2018 2017

Cover photo © Stock Connection Blue/Alamy Stock Photo
Typeset in Din Regular 12/14.4 pt. by Aptara, Inc.
Printed in the UK

A catalogue record for this title is available from the British Library

ISBN: 978 1 5104 1354 2

Introduction

Higher English

The course

The Higher English course aims to:

- provide you with the opportunity to develop listening, talking, reading and writing skills that will enable you to understand and use language
- develop your understanding of the complexities of language by studying a wide range of texts and building on your literacy skills
- develop high levels of analytical thinking and understanding of the impact of language.

How the award is graded

Your final grade for Higher English depends on three things:

- the two internal Unit Assessments you do in school or college: 'Analysis and Evaluation' and 'Creation and Production'; these don't count towards the final grade, but if you don't pass them, you cannot get a final grade – even if you sit and pass the exam
- your Portfolio of Writing; this is submitted in April for marking by SQA and counts for 30% of your final grade
- the exam you sit in May; that's what this book is all about.

The exams

Reading for Understanding, Analysis and Evaluation

- Exam time: 1 hour 30 minutes
- Total marks: 30
- Weighting in final grade: 30%
- What you have to do: read two passages and answer questions about the ideas and use of language in them.

Critical Reading

- Exam time: 1 hour 30 minutes
- Total marks: 40
- Weighting in final grade: 40%
- What you have to do: Section 1: read an extract from one of the Scottish Texts which are set for Higher and answer questions about it; Section 2: write an essay about a work of literature you have studied during your course.

1 Reading for Understanding, Analysis and Evaluation

Questions which ask for understanding (e.g. questions which say 'Identify ...' or 'Explain what ...' etc.)

- Keep your answers fairly short and pay attention to the number of marks available.
- Use your own words as far as possible. This means you mustn't just copy chunks from the passage – you have to show that you understand what it means by rephrasing it in your own words.

Questions about language features (e.g. questions which say 'Analyse how ...')

- This type of question will ask you to comment on features such as word choice, imagery, sentence structure, tone.
- You should pick out a relevant language feature and make a valid comment about its impact. Try to make your comments as specific as possible and avoid vague comments like 'It is a good word to use because it gives me a clear picture of what the writer is saying.' Remember that you will get no marks just for picking out a word or an image or a feature of sentence structure – it's the comment that counts.
- Some hints:
  - **word choice**: always try to pick a single word and then give its connotations, i.e. what it suggests
  - **sentence structure**: don't just name the feature – try to explain what effect it achieves in that particular sentence
  - **imagery**: try to explain what the image means literally and then go on to explain what the writer is trying to say by using that comparison
  - **tone**: this is always difficult – a good tip is to imagine the sentence or paragraph being read out loud and try to spot how the words or the structure give it a particular tone.

The last question

- Make sure you follow the instruction about whether you're looking for agreement or disagreement (or possibly both).
- When you start on Passage 2, you will have already answered several questions on Passage 1, so you should know its key ideas quite well; as you read Passage 2, try to spot important ideas in it which are similar or different (depending on the question).
- Stick to **key ideas** and don't include trivial ones; **three** relevant key ideas will usually be enough – your task is to decide what the most significant ones are.

2 Critical Reading

Section 1 – Scottish Text

The most important thing to remember here is that there are two very different types of question to be answered:

- three questions (for a total of 10 marks) which focus entirely on the extract
- one question (for 10 marks) which requires knowledge of the whole text (or of another poem or short story by the same writer).

The first type of question will often ask you to use the same type of close textual analysis skills you used in the Reading part of your Analysis and Evaluation Unit. The golden rules are to read each question very carefully and do exactly as instructed, and to remember that (just like the 'Analysis' questions in the Reading for Understanding, Analysis and Evaluation paper) there are no marks just for picking out a word or a feature – it's the comment that matters. While it is possible to score 2 marks for a good comment, you should try to make one comment for each mark available.

The second type of question requires you to identify common features (of theme and/or technique) in the extract and elsewhere in the writer's work. You can write a series of bullet points or a 'mini-essay', so choose the approach you feel more comfortable with.

A final bit of advice for the Scottish Text question: when you see the extract in the exam paper, don't get too confident just because you recognise it, because you certainly should recognise it if you've studied properly! And even if you've answered questions on it before, remember that the questions in the exam are likely to be different, so stay alert.

Section 2 – Critical Essay

A common mistake is to rely too heavily on ideas and whole paragraphs you have used in practice essays and try to use these for the question you have chosen in the exam. The trick is to come to the exam with lots of ideas and thoughts about at least one of the texts you have studied and use these to tackle the question you choose from the exam paper. You mustn't use the exam question as an excuse to trot out an answer you've prepared in advance.

Structure

Every good essay has a structure, but there is no 'correct' structure, no magic formula that the examiners are looking for. It's **your** essay, so structure it the way **you** want. As long as you're answering the question all the way through, then you'll be fine.

Relevance

Be relevant to the question **all the time** – not just in the first and last paragraphs.

Central Concerns

Try to make sure that your essay shows that you have thought about and understood the central concerns of the text, i.e. what it's 'about' – the ideas and themes the writer is exploring in the text.

Quotation

In poetry and drama essays, you're expected to quote from the text, but never fall into the trap of learning up a handful of quotations and forcing them all into the essay regardless of the question you're answering. In essays on a prose text, quotation is less important; you can show your knowledge more effectively by referring in detail to what happens in key sections of the novel or the short story.

Techniques

All the questions ask you to answer 'with reference to appropriate techniques', but this does not mean you'll get marks for simply naming techniques. The idea is to demonstrate your understanding of how various literary techniques work within a text, by referring to them in support of a key idea which is relevant to the question. Don't structure your whole essay around a list of techniques.

Revision grid

Reading for Understanding, Analysis and Evaluation

The grid below will help you focus on the different types of questions that feature in the RUAE paper. You can tick them off as you work through this book.

Question type	Paper A		Paper B		Paper C	
Understanding	1, 3a), 5		2, 3a), 4, 5		4a), 5	
Summary	6		1a)		1	
Analysis	2, 3b), 4		1b), 3b)		2, 3, 4b), 6 , 7*	
Evaluation	7		6		7*	
Comparison	8		7		8	

Critical Reading

It is not possible to focus in the same way on the skills for Critical Reading, but the grids below will allow you to keep a record of Scottish Text examples and Critical Essays you have worked on.

Scottish Text

Name of text	Date completed		
	Paper A	Paper B	Paper C

Critical Essay

Name of text	Paper	Question	Date

*Although Q7 begins 'Analyse', it has a joint 'Evaluation' listing on the revision grid as the question covers both areas.

Higher English

Paper 1: Reading for Understanding, Analysis and Evaluation

> **Duration: 90 minutes**
>
> **Total marks: 30**
>
> **Attempt ALL questions.**
>
> In the exam you must write your answers clearly in the answer booklet provided and clearly identify the question number you are attempting.
>
> Use **blue** or **black** ink.

The following two passages consider zoos and the treatment of wild animals.

Passage 1

Read the passage below and then attempt questions 1–7.

In the first passage, Janice Turner considers our attitudes to animal life in captivity.

How many rare gorillas are equal to a human life? To protect a three-year-old boy who fell into an enclosure at Cincinnati Zoo, keepers last week shot dead a 400lb silverback gorilla called Harambe. In a Chilean zoo last month, a suicidal man who clambered into the big cats' cage was saved at the expense of two lions.

5 That is how our scales of moral worth swing: a human is more precious than any number of animals. Who wouldn't wipe out a whole ape family to save your child, an entire species even? But you don't need to be an internet troll sniping 'they killed the wrong mammal' to feel repulsed. We lock up these wild creatures all their lives, then when a human trespasses into their prisons and they dare manifest natural behaviour, we shoot them dead.

10 What a travesty is a zoo. How can it still exist in civilised societies, this legacy of gentlemen collectors and capricious kings? We take our children to see animated taxidermy to reveal the glory of nature when it shows only our own stone hearts. I will never forget a bear I saw in Colchester Zoo: such a species is a solitary thing, who hides from view in the wild, but here he was exposed to gawping crowds, so in his boredom and anxiety he'd perform a series
15 of repetitive moves. Stand up, bend down, turn around. Over and over, all day. He was — in human terms — quite mad.

Oh, but zoos have evolved, I will be told. They moved the elephants out of London Zoo where they'd stand chained all day: great mammals who traverse a continent, pinioned on a grey concrete slab. After decades in which their immobility gave them arthritis, their lifespan was
20 half that of in the wild, they had less space than you'd allow a domestic cow and, in cooped-up despair, they killed a keeper.

Nowadays zoos have lavish landscaped enclosures, no heavy prison bars, to create the illusion of freedom. London Zoo has its 'Land of the Lions'. It has a ranger's hut, a mocked-up Indian railway station, a little high street with a barber's shop. It is there to reassure visitors
25 this is more natural and 'authentic', almost like the wild. But are lions really happier living in a cage that looks like a movie set?

Admittedly, the animal rights movement attracts a theocratic, purist cadre: the RSPCA activists who compare farming to the Holocaust; those more inclined to found donkey sanctuaries in Syria than care for suffering children; those who argue that animals should
30 have representation in parliament. For these people the moral scales balance: animal and human life have equal value. Yet beyond this often angry fringe are people like me, a happy meat-eater who isn't even particularly fond of dogs, but who can't in conscience see wild animals as exhibits, specimens, playthings.

A decade ago, I took my kids to SeaWorld in San Diego to watch the orcas perform. I booked
35 tickets without thinking. It was the stuff of sunny childhood TV shows: happy whales, leaping and splashing, 'kissing' their keepers. Except that watching it live you'd have to turn off half your brain not to feel queasy, to wonder how these mighty and intelligent animals enjoyed living in tiny tanks not open oceans.

A recent documentary *Blackfish* followed the case of a male orca at SeaWorld called Tilikum:
40 his capture as a baby, the dark solitary conditions in which whales are transported, how this perversion of their nature sends them psychotic until eventually Tilikum ate his keeper. After this, SeaWorld attendance plummeted. The theme park has announced it will no longer breed orcas and the live shows will be phased out. Public tastes shifted.

The broad arc of human progress has a parallel animal ark. Bear-baiting, dog-fighting,
45 circuses, chimps' tea parties were all once normal, innocent, fun. Yet each generation is a little kinder to other creatures. The furore about the killing of Cecil the Lion on a 'trophy hunt' in Zimbabwe was not media-led hysteria. Rather it was mass shock that an ordinary guy, a dentist from Minnesota, would get pleasure from destroying such a creature. You could understand an impoverished African poacher. But didn't that impulse to 'bag' beasts,
50 to measure your manhood against your obliteration of fur and ivory, to pose beside a tiger's corpse with a goofy grin, die out in the nineteenth century? Apparently not: lions and other big game are bred just for the thrill of humans killing them for trophy hunts in southern Africa, a lucrative business that purports to conserve as it trades in death.

Zoos too have their dark underside. As with the famous public dissection of Marius,
55 a perfectly healthy giraffe at Copenhagen Zoo, they think nothing of slaughtering an inconvenient 'surplus' of lions or elephants. Their conservation work, the protection of very rare species may be valuable. But how can zoos still justify keeping polar bears, great apes and tigers, who fare badly in captivity but as 'charismatic megafauna' are good for profits?

It is time for these melancholy mammal museums to die out. Let kids watch wildlife
60 documentaries on TV: in real life, they are just as excited to meet a snake or a giant spider. The species scale is tipping. Costa Rica has become the first country to disband all its zoos and sent its animals to conservation parks. Why shouldn't Britain be next?

Passage 2

Read the passage below and attempt question 8. While reading, you may wish to make notes on the main ideas and/or highlight key points in the passage.

The second passage comes from the website of PETA (People for the Ethical Treatment of Animals). For the most up-to-date information about animals used in entertainment, visit peta.org.

Zoos evolved at a time when travel for most people was impractical. Nowadays, wildlife watchers can hop on a plane to Africa or Australia for photo safaris or even stay at home and catch nature documentaries on television or view live Internet video feeds, which capture animals' natural behaviour that is rarely, if ever, seen in zoos. Zoos once boasted
5 attendance of over a hundred million each year. Now, however, attendance at some zoos are dropping. This is likely because these zoos are of declining interest to a public that has become much more knowledgeable about the needs and behaviour of wild animals and is more aware of the toll that captivity takes on animals who are meant to roam free.

There is no excuse for keeping intelligent, social animals in cages for our fleeting distraction
10 and amusement. Habitat loss and other perils of the wild are not prevented by confining animals in cramped conditions and depriving them of everything that is natural and important to them.

Most zoo exhibits provide animals with little, if any, opportunity to express natural behaviour or make choices in their daily lives, and this can lead to boredom and neurosis. With nothing
15 to do, animals in zoos may sleep too much, eat too much, and exhibit behaviour that is rarely, if ever, seen in the wild. Primates sometimes throw faeces and engage in 'regurgitation and reingestion' — vomiting and then consuming the vomit.

Wide-ranging animals such as bears and big cats often pace incessantly. Primates and birds may mutilate themselves, and chimpanzees and gorillas can become overly aggressive.
20 Hooved animals sometimes lick and chew on fences and make strange lip, neck, and tongue movements. Giraffes may twist their necks, bending their heads back and forth repeatedly. Elephants frequently bob their heads and sway from side to side.

Marine mammals repeatedly swim in the same repetitious patterns in their tanks. Fish suffer too. A study conducted by the Captive Animals' Protection Society concluded that 90 percent
25 of public aquariums studied had animals that showed stereotypic (neurotic) behaviour, such as interacting with transparent boundaries, repeatedly raising their heads above the surface of the water, spinning around an imaginary object, and frequently turning on one side and rubbing along the floor of the tank.

By their very nature, zoos leave animals vulnerable to a variety of dangers from which they
30 have no defence or opportunity to escape. Animals in zoos have been poisoned, left to starve, deprived of veterinary care, and burned alive in fires. Many have died after eating coins, plastic bags, and other items thrown into their cages. Animals have been beaten, bludgeoned, and stolen by people who were able to gain access to their exhibits. A bear starved to death at the Toledo Zoo after zoo officials locked her up to hibernate without food or water — not
35 knowing that her species doesn't hibernate. At the Niabi Zoo in Illinois, a 3-month-old lion cub was euthanized after his spinal cord was crushed by a falling exhibit door. Despite knowing that two Asiatic bears had fought dozens of times, the Denver Zoo continued to house them together until one finally killed the other.

Marine-mammal facilities are part of a billion-dollar industry built on the suffering of
40 intelligent, social beings who are denied everything that is natural and important to them. In the wild, orcas and members of other dolphin species live in large, intricate social groups and swim vast distances every day in the open ocean. In aquariums and marine parks, these animals can only swim endless circles in enclosures that to them are like bathtubs and are unable to engage in most natural behaviours. They are forced to perform silly tricks for food
45 and are frequently torn away from family members as they're shuffled between parks. The chronic and debilitating stress of captivity can weaken their immune systems, causing them to die earlier than their wild counterparts — even though they are safe from predators and receive regular meals and veterinary care.

Questions

1 Read lines 1–9. Using your own words as far as possible, explain the key points made in these lines about our attitudes to animal life.

2

2 Read lines 10–16. By referring to **at least two** examples, analyse how the writer's use of language makes clear her disapproval of zoos.

4

3 Read lines 17–26.

    a) Using your own words as far as possible, explain what London Zoo has done to try to improve its treatment of animals.

2

    b) Analyse how the writer's use of language casts doubt on the validity of this change in approach.

2

4 Read lines 27–33. By referring to **at least two** examples, analyse how the writer's use of language creates a negative impression of the animal rights movement.

4

5 Read lines 34–43. Explain how the writer uses the example of the orcas at SeaWorld to develop her argument.

3

6 Read lines 44–58. Using your own words as far as possible, summarise the key points in the writer's argument in these lines.

5

7 Evaluate the effectiveness of the last paragraph (lines 59–62) as a conclusion to the passage as a whole.

3

Question on both passages

8 Look at both passages. Both writers express their views about zoos and the treatment of wild animals.

Identify **three** key areas on which they agree. You should support the points by referring to important ideas in both passages.

You may answer this question in continuous prose or in a series of developed bullet points.

5

[End of question paper]

Paper 2: Critical Reading

Duration: 90 minutes

Total marks: 40

Section 1 – Scottish Text – 20 marks

Read an extract from a Scottish text you have previously studied and attempt the questions.

Choose ONE text from either

Part A – Drama   Pages 9–13

or

Part B – Prose   Pages 14–20

or

Part C – Poetry   Pages 21–29

Attempt ALL questions for your chosen text.

Section 2 – Critical Essay – 20 marks

Attempt ONE question from the following genres – Drama, Prose Fiction, Prose Non-Fiction, Poetry, Film and Television Drama, or Language.

Your answer must be on a different genre from that chosen in Section 1.

You should spend approximately 45 minutes on each Section.

In the exam you must write your answers clearly in the answer booklet provided and clearly identify the question number you are attempting.

Use **blue** or **black** ink.

Section 1 – Scottish Text – 20 marks

Choose ONE text from Drama, Prose or Poetry.

Read the text extract carefully and then attempt ALL the questions for your chosen text.

You should spend about 45 minutes on this Section.

Part A – Scottish Text – Drama

Text 1 – Drama

If you choose this text you may not attempt a question on Drama in Section 2.

Read the extract below and then attempt the following questions.

The Slab Boys by John Byrne

This extract is from near the beginning of Act One.

	(*Enter* WILLIE CURRY)	
	CURRY:	Ha ... there you are, McCann. Where've you been this morning? Farrell there said you were unwell.
	PHIL:	Er ... um ... yes ...
5	CURRY:	C'mon, what was up with you?
	PHIL:	Er ... touch of the ... er ... drawhaw.
	CURRY:	The what?
	PHIL:	Dee-oh-raw-ho ... the skitters ... it was very bad.
	CURRY:	Why didn't you come to me earlier? I could've got Nurse to have a look at you ...
10	PHIL:	No ... it's not what ye'd cry a 'spectator sport', Mr Curly ...
	CURRY:	In future you report all illnesses to me ... first thing. How am I supposed to keep tabs on you lot if I don't know where the devil you are?
	PHIL:	Ah wis down the lavvies ...
	CURRY:	You wouldn't get much done down there ...
15	PHIL:	Oh, I wouldn't say that, Mr Corrie ...
	CURRY:	Godstruth, I don't know ... If I'd had you chaps out in Burma. Diarrhoea? There were men in my platoon fighting the Japanese with dysentery.
	SPANKY:	How did they fire it ... from chip baskets?
20	CURRY:	Less of your damned cheek, Farrell. A couple of years in the Forces would smarten your ideas up a bit ... they'd soon have those silly duck's arse haircuts off you. And what have I told you about bringing that bloody contraption in ... eh?
	SPANKY:	What contraption?
	CURRY:	How do you expect to get any work done with that racket going on?
25	SPANKY:	Pardon?
	CURRY:	Whoever owns this gadget can ask Mr Barton for it back. (*Protests from boys*) I'll be calling back in five minutes and if you bunch are still lounging about you're for the high jump, understand? Now, get on with it ... (*Exits*)

Questions

MARKS

1   Look at lines 1–7. Analyse how the dramatist presents Curry as an overbearing character in these lines.

2

2   Look at lines 8–18. By referring to at least **two** examples, analyse how the humour in these lines relies on deliberate misunderstanding of what Curry has said.

4

3   Look at lines 19–28. By referring to at least **two** examples, analyse how the writer's use of language in these lines conveys Curry's dislike of the Slab Boys and their lifestyle.

4

4   By referring to this extract and to elsewhere in the play, discuss the characterisation of Willie Curry.

10

OR

Text 2 – Drama

If you choose this text you may not attempt a question on Drama in Section 2.
Read the extract below and then attempt the following questions.

The Cheviot, the Stag and the Black, Black Oil by John McGrath

In this extract the roots of the Highland Clearances are explained.

(GAELIC SINGER *is singing a quiet Jacobite song in Gaelic*)

MC: It begins, I suppose, with 1746 – Culloden and all that. The Highlands were in a bit of a mess. Speaking – or singing – the Gaelic language was forbidden. (*Singing stops.*) Wearing the plaid was forbidden. (SINGER *takes off her plaid, sits.*) Things were all set for a change. So Scene One – Strathnaver 1813.

5

Drum roll. Page of book turned, a cottage pops up from in between the next two pages.
Enter two Strathnaver girls, singing.

GIRLS: Hé mandu's truagh nach tigeadh

10   Hé mandu siod 'gam iarraidh

                Hé mandu gille's litir

                He ri oro each is diollaid

                Heman dubh hi ri oro

                Hó ró hù ó

15 *As they sing, a YOUNG HIGHLANDER comes on, watches them, talks to audience.*

YH: The women were great at making it all seem fine. But it was no easy time to be alive in. Sir John Sinclair of Caithness had invented the Great Sheep; that is to say, he had introduced the Cheviot to the North. Already in Assynt the Sutherland family

20   had cleared the people off their land – and the people were not too pleased about it.

FIRST WOMAN:	Ach blethers –	
SECOND WOMAN:	Ha chuir iad dragh oirnne co diubh. (They won't bother us here.)	

25 FIRST WOMAN: The Countess has always been very kind to us.

YH: Aye, and she's away in England.

FIRST WOMAN: Why wouldn't she be?

YH: With her fancy palaces and feasts for Kings and fine French wines – and it's our rent she's spending.

30 FIRST WOMAN: Rent! You never pay any rent –

YH: Where would I get the money to pay rent? (*To audience.*) If it's not bad weather flattening the barley, it's mildew in the potatoes, and last year it was both together ... And now they're talking about bringing in soldiers to clear us off the land

35 completely ...

SECOND WOMAN: Saighdearan? De mu dheidhinn saighdearan? (Soldiers – what do you mean, soldiers?)

YH: There were one hundred and fifty of them arrived in a boat off Lochinver.

40 FIRST WOMAN: Would you get on with some work?

SECOND WOMAN: Seo-lion an cogan. (Here fill up the bucket.)

They sing on, as YH goes to a corner of the cottage to pee in the bucket. They watch him and laugh. Suddenly he panics, does up his trousers and rushes over.

YH: Here – there's a couple of gentlemen coming up the strath.

45 FIRST WOMAN: Gentlemen?

YH: (*to audience*) The two gentlemen were James Loch and Patrick Sellar, factor and under-factor to the Sutherland estates.

FIRST WOMAN: Oh, look at the style of me ...

YH: (*handing them the bucket*) You might find a good use for this.

50 (*Goes.*)

Questions

5   Look at lines 1–21. By referring to at least **two** examples, analyse how the playwright creates a relaxed mood in these lines.

4

6   Look at lines 22–40. By referring to at least **two** examples, analyse how the difference in outlook between the Young Highlander and the two Women is conveyed.

4

7   By referring to lines 41–50, explain how the extract ends on a humorous note.

2

8   The staging of *The Cheviot, the Stag and the Black, Black Oil* is very different from that of a conventional play. By referring to this extract and to elsewhere in the play, discuss how effective you find this unconventional staging in exploring at least one key idea in the play.

10

OR

Text 3 – Drama

If you choose this text you may not attempt a question on Drama in Section 2.

Read the extract below and then attempt the following questions.

Men Should Weep by Ena Lamont Stewart

In this extract from near the end of Act One, Jenny leaves home.

	MAGGIE:	I dinna ken whit way we bring weans intae the world at a. Slavin an worryin for them a yer days, an naethin but heartbreak at the end o it.
5	ALEC:	Aw, come on Ma, cheer up. (*He smooths her hair: she looks up at him gratefully, lovingly, and lays his hand to her cheek. Isa looks at them and laughs.*)
	ISA:	Mammy's big tumphy! G'on, ye big lump o dough!
		Alec disengages himself from his mother and grins feebly.
10	LILY:	My, you're a right bitch, Isa. Yin o they days you'll get whit's comin tae ye. Alec's no as saft as he looks.
	ISA:	Is he no, Auntie? I'm right gled tae hear it.
		Jenny comes in with a suitcase.
	JENNY:	Well, I'm awa. Cheeribye, everybody.
	LILY:	Goodbye. And good riddance tae bad rubbish.
15		*Jenny sticks out her tongue.*
	MAGGIE:	Jenny, whit am I goin tae tell folks?
	JENNY:	Folks? Ye mean the neighbours? If they've got the impidence tae ask, tell them it's nane o their bloomin business.
	MAGGIE:	Oh Jenny, Jenny! Whit's happened tae ye, Jenny?

20	JENNY:	Whit's happened? I've wakened up, that's whit's happened. There's better places than this. Jist because I wis born here disnae mean I've got tae bide here.
	LILY:	Gie yer Mammy a kiss.
	JENNY:	(*She wavers for a moment, then tosses her head*) I'm no in the
25		mood for kissin. Cheerio, Isa. Mind whit I tellt ye.
	ALEC:	Aboot whit? (*He creeps forward, suspiciously to Isa*) Whit did she tell ye, eh?
	ISA:	(*Pushing his face away*) A bed-time story; but no for wee boys.
		Maggie looks helplessly on, combing her hair with her fingers.
30	LILY:	Clear aff then, if ye're gaun!
	ISA:	Ta ta, Jenny. See you roon the toon.
	JENNY:	Aye. Ta ta.
		The door opens. John comes in. He and Jenny look at each other.
	JOHN:	(*Wretched*) I thought ye'd hev gone.
35	JENNY:	Naw. Jist gaun.
		He lowers his eyes from her face and stands aside to let her pass. He turns and watches her from the doorway until her footsteps die away and the outside door bangs.

Questions

MARKS

9   Look at lines 1–31.

    a) By referring to at least **two** examples in these lines, analyse how the playwright conveys Maggie's state of mind to the audience.   4

    b) Analyse how the playwright makes the audience aware of Isa's character in these lines.   2

10 By referring to at least **two** examples, explain why the end of the extract (lines 32–38) would be very dramatic in performance.   4

11 By referring to this extract and to elsewhere in the play, discuss how Maggie changes in the course of the play.   10

Part B – Scottish Text – Prose

Text 1 – Prose

If you choose this text you may not attempt a question on Prose in Section 2.

Read the extract below and then attempt the following questions.

The Red Door by Iain Crichton Smith

The extract is from near the end of The Red Door.

But really was he happy? That was the question. When he considered it carefully he knew that he wasn't. He didn't like eating alone, he didn't like sitting in the house alone, he didn't like having none who belonged to him, to whom he could tell his secret thoughts, for example that such and such was a mean devil and that that other one was an ungrateful rat.

5 He had to keep a perpetually smiling face to the world, that was his trouble. But the red door didn't do that. It was foreign and confident. It seemed to be saying what it was, not what it thought others expected it to say. On the other hand, he didn't like wellingtons and a fisherman's jersey. He hated them in fact: they had no elegance.

Now Mary had elegance. Though she was a bit odd, she had elegance. It was true that the
10 villagers didn't understand her but that was because she read many books, her father having been a teacher. And on the other hand she made no concessions to anybody. She seemed to be saying, 'You can take me or leave me.' She never gossiped. She was proud and distant. She had a world of her own. She paid for everything on the nail. She was quite well off. But her world was her own, depending on none.

15 She was very fond of children and used to make up masks for them at Hallowe'en. As well as this she would walk by herself at night, which argued that she was romantic. And it was said that she had sudden bursts of rage which too might be the sign of a spirit without servility. One couldn't marry a clod.

Murdo stared at the door and as he looked at it he seemed to be drawn inside it into its deep
20 caves with all sorts of veins and passages. It was like a magic door out of the village but at the same time it pulsed with a deep red light which made it appear alive. It was all very odd and very puzzling, to think that a red door could make such a difference to house and moors and streams.

Solid and heavy he stood in front of it in his wellingtons, scratching his head. But the red door
25 was not a mirror and he couldn't see himself in it. Rather he was sucked into it as if it were a place of heat and colour and reality. But it was different and it was his.

It was true that the villagers when they woke would see it and perhaps make fun of it, and would advise him to repaint it. They might not even want him in the village if he insisted on having a red door. Still they could all have red doors if they wanted to. Or they could hunt him
30 out of the village.

Questions

12 Look at lines 1–14. By referring to at least **two** examples, analyse how the sentence structure in these lines helps to convey Murdo's feelings.

4

13 By referring to lines 15–18, describe Murdo's attitude to Mary.

2

14 Look at lines 19–30. By referring to at least **two** examples, analyse how the writer's use of language in these lines suggests the door has mystical qualities.

4

15 By referring to this story and to at least one other by Crichton Smith, discuss to what extent you feel pity for characters he creates.

10

OR

Text 2 – Prose

If you choose this text you may not attempt a question on Prose in Section 2.

Read the extract below and then attempt the following questions.

A Time to Keep by George Mackay Brown

I was baiting a line with mussels at the end of the house when I saw the black car coming between the hills and stopping where the road ended at the mouth of the valley. It was the first car ever seen in the island, a Ford.

A small, neat man with a beard and a watch-chain across his belly got out and
5 came stepping briskly up our side of the valley.

'Ingi,' I shouted, 'your father's here.'

She was baking, going between the table, the cupboard, and the fire, a blue reek all about her.

But now all thought of bread was forgotten. She let out a cry of distress. She
10 threw off her mealy apron, she filled a bowl of water and dipped face and hands in it and wiped herself dry with the towel. She put the text straight on the wall. She covered my six rationalist books with a cloth. She fell to combing her hair and twisting it into a new bright knot at the back of her head. All the same, the house was full of the blue hot reek of baking. And the bed was unmade. And
15 there was a litter of fish-guts and crab toes about the door. She tried hard, Ingi, but she was not the tidiest of the croft women.

Ingi came and stood at the door.

As for me, I went on with my lines. I was not beholden to him.

Mr Sinclair, merchant in Osmundwall – and forby kirk elder, Justice of the
20 Peace, chairman of the district council – stood at the corner of the barn.

'Father,' said Ingi.

'My girl,' said Mr Sinclair. He touched her gently on the arm.

'Well, Bill,' he said to me.

'Well,' I said.

25 'Father, I'm glad to see you,' said Ingi.

'No happier than I am to see you,' said Mr Sinclair. 'Ingi,' said he, 'you're not looking well. Not at all well. What way is it that we haven't seen you for three whole months, eh? Ingi, I doubt you're working too hard, is that it?'

'On a croft,' I said, 'everybody must work.'

30 'Is that so, Bill?' said Mr Sinclair. 'Maybe so. At the present moment I'm speaking to Ingi, to my daughter. I'll be wanting to speak to you later, before I go.'

'Say what you have to say now,' I said, 'for I have work to do.'

'Bill,' said Ingi unhappily.

'Work to do, is that it, work to do,' said Mr Sinclair. 'Then if you have so much 35 work to do, why don't you give my daughter enough money for her to live on? Eh? Just answer me. Why don't you do that? Last month you cut down on her money. The van man told me. She couldn't buy jam or paraffin. Don't imagine I don't hear things.'

Questions

MARKS

16 Look at lines 1–20. Explain how the writer makes the reader aware of:

   a)   Bill's feelings for Sinclair   2

   b)   Ingi's feelings for Sinclair   2

   c)   Bill's feelings for Ingi.   2

17 Look at lines 21–38. By referring to at least **two** examples, analyse how the writer's use of language in these lines conveys the tension between Bill and Sinclair.   4

18 By referring to *A Time to Keep* and to at least one other story by Mackay Brown, discuss the way he creates tension at key moments in his stories.   10

OR

Text 3 – Prose

If you choose this text you may not attempt a question on Prose in Section 2.

Read the extract below and then attempt the following questions.

The Trick Is To Keep Breathing by Janice Galloway

This extract is from midway through the interview with 'Dr One' before Joy is admitted to hospital.

Time for questions about my work. Asinine things: my colleagues and how to organise the day to be under less pressure, my family and how they could be a source of help. My family. This little man with the pink head and dandruff showing through, his tortoise neck rising and falling reaching to my gullet.

5 I clenched my wet fists and glared. What did he think he was here to do for christsake? He knew nothing. He was just a little man being paid to sit here and say the first thing that came into his bald head, rooting for the meaningless nothings that made the life of a complete stranger. It wasn't honest. He didn't understand how little any of this mattered. How little either of us mattered.

10 Contempt gave me a boost. The scored arteries on my wrist throbbed, pulsing with the adrenalin of imminent danger. I felt like an empty tiger. I hoped he knew.

Why are you smiling Miss Stone?

He squinted across the table through those readjusted spectacles.

Why are you smiling?

15 Didn't he know? He was stuck in this stuffy room in the corner of a psychiatric ward, talking about things of no consequence with an equally absurd stranger, hiding from the sun behind this hideous hemp curtain and he couldn't see it. The sky was passing outside for chrissakes. Planes and birds. People going about their work. The whole thing was insane. I tried a sardonic laugh but it

20 didn't work: bits got stuck on the way out so it sounded more like a cough. I let my head hang back and sighed instead. The rush of blood made me abruptly dizzy. He carried on regardless saying something in the background but it was just a blur. Tears drained backward into my ears. I was floating up toward the ceiling, inflating with something like love: serene and distant as the Virgin Mary,

25 radiating Truth from the halo of stars round my head. I knew so much,

There was No Point.
Everything was the Same as Nothing.
And I knew there was nothing he could say.

Questions

19 Look at lines 1–11. By referring to at least **two** examples, analyse how the writer's use of language in these lines conveys Joy's contempt for the doctor.

4

20 Look at lines 15–25. By referring to at least **two** examples, analyse how the writer's use of language in these lines makes the reader aware of Joy's disturbed state of mind.

4

21 What impression of Joy is created by lines 26–28?

2

22 By referring to this extract and to elsewhere in the novel, discuss how the novelist explores Joy's alienation from those around her.

10

OR

Text 4 – Prose

If you choose this text you may not attempt a question on Prose in Section 2.

Read the extract below and then attempt the following questions.

Sunset Song by Lewis Grassic Gibbon

In this extract from Part IV (Harvest), Ewan has returned on leave from the army.

Drunk he had come from the station and more than two hours late. Standing at last in the kitchen in his kilts he'd looked round and sneered *Hell, Chris, what a bloody place!* as she ran to him. And he'd flung his pack one way and his hat the other and kissed her as though she were a tink, his hands on her as quickly
5 as that, hot and questing and wise as his hands had never been. She saw the hot smoulder fire in his eyes then, but no blush on his face, it was red with other things. But she smothered her horror and laughed, and kissed him and struggled from him, and cried *Ewan, who's this?*

Young Ewan held back, shy-like, staring, and just said *It's father.* At that the
10 strange, swaying figure in the tartan kilts laughed, coarse-like, *Well, we'll hope so, eh Chris? Any supper left – unless you're too bloody stand-offish even to have that?*

She couldn't believe her own ears. *Stand-offish? Oh, Ewan!* and ran to him again, but he shook her away, *Och, all right, I'm wearied. For Christ's sake let a man sit down.* He staggered to the chair she'd made ready for him, a picture-book of
15 young Ewan's lay there, he picked the thing up and flung it to the other side of the room, and slumped down into the chair. *Hell, what a blasted climb to a blasted place. Here, give us some tea.*

She sat beside him to serve him, she knew her face had gone white. But she poured the tea and spread the fine supper she'd been proud to make, it might
20 hardly have been there for the notice he paid it, drinking cup after cup of the tea like a beast at a trough. She saw him clearer then, the coarse hair that sprang like short bristles all over his head, the neck with its red and angry circle about

the collar of the khaki jacket, a great half-healed scar across the back of his hand glinted putrescent blue. Suddenly his eyes came on her, *Well, damn't, is that*
25 *all you've to say to me now I've come home? I'd have done better to spend the night with a tart in the town.*

She didn't say anything, she couldn't, the tears were choking in her throat and smarting and biting at her eyelids, pressing to come, the tears that she'd sworn she'd never shed all the time he was home on leave. And she didn't dare look
30 at him lest he should see, but he saw and pushed back his chair and got up in a rage, *God Almighty, what are you snivelling about now? You always were snivelling, I mind.* And out he went, young Ewan ran to her side and flung his arms round her, *Mother, don't cry, I don't like him, he's a tink, that soldier!*

Questions

23 Look at lines 1–17. By referring to at least **two** examples, analyse how the writer's use of language in these lines shows the offensiveness of Ewan's behaviour.

4

24 Look at lines 18–26. By referring to at least **two** examples, analyse how the writer makes the reader aware of Chris's perception of Ewan.

4

25 By referring to the whole extract, describe the change in young Ewan's reaction to his father.

2

26 By referring to this extract and to elsewhere in the novel, discuss the development of the relationship between Chris and Ewan.

10

OR

Text 5 – Prose

If you choose this text you may not attempt a question on Prose in Section 2.
Read the extract below and then attempt the following questions.

The Cone-Gatherers by Robin Jenkins

This extract is from early in Chapter 1. The brothers are getting ready to climb down from the tree after a day gathering cones.

The time came when, thrilling as a pipe lament across the water, daylight announced it must go: there was a last blaze of light, an uncanny clarity, a splendour and puissance; and then the abdication began. Single stars appeared, glittering in a sky pale and austere. Dusk like a breathing drifted in among the
5 trees and crept over the loch. Slowly the mottled yellow of the chestnuts, the bronze of beech, the saffron of birches, all the magnificent sombre harmonies of decay, became indistinguishable. Owls hooted. A fox barked.

It was past time to climb down and go home. The path to the earth was unfamiliar; in the dark it might be dangerous. Once safely down, they would
10 have to find their way like ghosts to their hut in the heart of the wood. Yet Neil did not give the word to go down. It was not zeal to fill the bags that made him linger, for he had given up gathering. He just sat, motionless and silent; and his brother, accustomed to these trances, waited in sympathy: he was sure that even at midnight he could climb down any tree, and help Neil to climb down too. He
15 did not know what Neil was thinking, and never asked; even if told he would not understand. It was enough that they were together.

For about half an hour they sat there, no longer working. The scent of the tree seemed to strengthen with the darkness, until Calum fancied he was resting in the heart of an enormous flower. As he breathed in the fragrance, he stroked the
20 branches, and to his gentle hands they were as soft as petals. More owls cried. Listening, as if he was an owl himself, he saw in imagination the birds huddled on branches far lower than this one on which he sat. He became an owl himself, he rose and fanned his wings, flew close to the ground, and then swooped, to rise again with vole or shrew squeaking in his talons. Part-bird then, part-man,
25 he suffered in the ineluctable predicament of necessary pain and death. The owl could not be blamed; it lived according to its nature; but its victim must be pitied. This was the terrifying mystery, why creatures he loved should kill one another. He had been told that all over the world in the war now being fought men, women, and children were being slaughtered in thousands; cities were
30 being burnt down. He could not understand it, and so he tried, with success, to forget it.

'Well, we'd better make for down,' said Neil at last, with a heavy sigh.

'I could sit up here all night, Neil,' his brother assured him eagerly.

Questions

27 Look at lines 1–7. By referring to at least **two** examples, analyse how the writer's use of language in these lines creates a vivid atmosphere.

4

28 Look at lines 8–16. Explain the relationship between Calum and Neil which is revealed in these lines.

2

29 Look at lines 17–33. By referring to at least **two** examples, analyse how the writer reveals aspects of Calum's character in these lines.

4

30 By referring to the extract and to elsewhere in the novel, discuss how Jenkins portrays Calum's innocence.

10

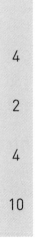

Part C – Scottish Text – Poetry

Text 1 – Poetry

If you choose this text you may not attempt a question on Poetry in Section 2.
Read the extract below and then attempt the following questions.

A Poet's Welcome to His Love-Begotten Daughter by Robert Burns

Thou's welcome, wean; mishanter fa' me,
If thoughts o' thee, or yet thy mamie,
Shall ever daunton me or awe me,
My bonie lady,
5 Or if I blush when thou shalt ca' me
Tyta or daddie.

Tho' now they ca' me fornicator,
An' tease my name in kintry clatter,
The mair they talk, I'm kent the better,
10 E'en let them clash;
An auld wife's tongue's a feckless matter
To gie ane fash.

Welcome! my bonie, sweet, wee dochter,
Tho' ye come here a wee unsought for,
15 And tho' your comin' I hae fought for,
Baith kirk and queir;
Yet, by my faith, ye're no unwrought for,
That I shall swear!

Wee image o' my bonie Betty,
20 As fatherly I kiss and daut thee,
As dear, and near my heart I set thee
Wi' as gude will
As a' the priests had seen me get thee
That's out o' hell.

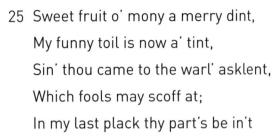

25 Sweet fruit o' mony a merry dint,

My funny toil is now a' tint,

Sin' thou came to the warl' asklent,

Which fools may scoff at;

In my last plack thy part's be in't

30 The better ha'f o't.

Questions

31 Look at lines 1–12. By referring to at least **two** examples, analyse how the poet's language in these lines creates a contrast between his attitude to his daughter and his attitude to those who criticise him.

4

32 Look at lines 13–18. Analyse how the sentence structure in these lines creates a defiant tone.

2

33 Look at lines 19–30. By referring to at least **two** examples in these lines, analyse how the poet's language conveys the depth of his love for his daughter.

4

34 By referring to this poem and to at least one other by Burns, discuss his use of contrast to explore important ideas.

10

OR

Text 2 – Poetry

If you choose this text you may not attempt a question on Poetry in Section 2.
Read the extract below and then attempt the following questions.

Mrs Midas by Carol Ann Duffy

It was late September. I'd just poured a glass of wine, begun

to unwind, while the vegetables cooked. The kitchen

filled with the smell of itself, relaxed, its steamy breath

gently blanching the windows. So I opened one,

5 then with my fingers wiped the other's glass like a brow.

He was standing under the pear tree snapping a twig.

Now the garden was long and the visibility poor, the way

the dark of the ground seems to drink the light of the sky,

but that twig in his hand was gold. And then he plucked

10   a pear from a branch – we grew Fondante d'Automne –

and it sat in his palm like a light bulb. On.

I thought to myself, Is he putting fairy lights in the tree?

He came into the house. The doorknobs gleamed.

He drew the blinds. You know the mind; I thought of

15   the Field of the Cloth of Gold and of Miss Macready.

He sat in that chair like a king on a burnished throne.

The look on his face was strange, wild, vain. I said,

What in the name of God is going on? He started to laugh.

I served up the meal. For starters, corn on the cob.

20   Within seconds he was spitting out the teeth of the rich.

He toyed with his spoon, then mine, then with the knives, the forks.

He asked where was the wine. I poured with a shaking hand,

a fragrant, bone-dry white from Italy, then watched

as he picked up the glass, goblet, golden chalice, drank.

Questions

35 Look at lines 1–6. By referring to at least **two** examples, analyse how the poet's language creates an ordinary, everyday atmosphere in these lines.

4

36 Look at lines 7–12. Analyse how the poet's language conveys the confusion that is beginning to arise in the speaker's mind.

2

37 Look at lines 13–24. By referring to at least **two** examples, analyse how the poet's language conveys the strangeness of the husband's behaviour.

4

38 By referring to this poem and at least one other by Duffy, discuss how she introduces unusual or surprising ideas into her poems.

10

A

OR

Text 3 – Poetry

If you choose this text you may not attempt a question on Poetry in Section 2.
Read the poem below and then attempt the following questions.

Some Old Photographs by Liz Lochhead

weather evocative as scent

the romance of dark stormclouds

in big skies over the low wide river

    of long shadows and longer shafts of light

5   of smoke

    fabulous film-noir stills of Central Station

of freezing fog silvering the chilled, stilled parks

    of the glamorous past

    where drops on a rainmate are sequins

10   in the lamplight, in the black-and-white

    your young, still-lovely mother laughs, the

    hem of her sundress whipped up

    by a wind on a beach before you were even born

    all the Dads in hats

15 are making for Central at five past five

in the snow, in the rain, in the sudden *what-a-scorcher*,

in the smog, their

belted dark overcoats white-spattered by the starlings

    starlings swarming

20 in that perfect and permanent cloud

above what was

never really this photograph

but always all the passing now

and noise and stink and smoky breath of George Square

25 wee boays, a duchess, bunting, there's a

big launch on the Clyde

and that boat is yet to sail

Questions

39 Look at lines 1–10. By referring to at least **two** examples, analyse how the poet's language creates a dream-like atmosphere in these lines.

4

40 Look at lines 11–18. Analyse how the poet reminds the reader in these lines that these photographs are old.

2

41 Look at lines 19–24. By referring to at least **two** examples, analyse how the poet's language creates a vivid impression of George Square.

4

42 By referring to this poem and to at least one other poem by Lochhead, discuss how she explores the passage of time.

10

OR

Text 4 – Poetry

If you choose this text you may not attempt a question on Poetry in Section 2.

Read the poem below and then attempt the following questions.

Memorial by Norman MacCaig

Everywhere she dies. Everywhere I go she dies.

No sunrise, no city square, no lurking beautiful mountain

but has her death in it.

The silence of her dying sounds through

5 the carousel of language. It's a web

on which laughter stitches itself. How can my hand

clasp another's when between them

is that thick death, that intolerable distance?

She grieves for my grief. Dying, she tells me

10 that bird dives from the sun, that fish

leaps into it. No crocus is carved more gently

than the way her dying

shapes my mind. – But I hear, too,
the other words,

15   black words that make the sound
of soundlessness, that name the nowhere
she is continuously going into.

Ever since she died
she can't stop dying. She makes me

20   her elegy. I am a walking masterpiece,
a true fiction
of the ugliness of death.
I am her sad music.

Questions

43 Look at lines 4–6. ('The silence … stitches itself.') Analyse how the poet's imagery in these lines conveys how the speaker has been affected by the death.

2

44 Look at lines 9–17. By referring to at least **two** examples, analyse how the poet uses contrast in these lines to reveal the speaker's feelings.

4

45 Look at lines 18–23. By referring to at least **two** examples, analyse how the poet conveys in these lines the impact the death has had on the speaker.

4

46 By referring to this poem and to at least one other by MacCaig, discuss his exploration of deeply emotional situations.

10

OR

Text 5 – Poetry

If you choose this text you may not attempt a question on Poetry in Section 2.
Read the extract below and then attempt the following questions.

Hallaig by Sorley MacLean

In Screapadal of my people
where Norman and Big Hector were,
their daughters and their sons are a wood
going up beside the stream.

5 Proud tonight the pine cocks

crowing on the top of Cnoc an Ra,

straight their backs in the moonlight –

they are not the wood I love.

I will wait for the birch wood

10 until it comes up by the cairn,

until the whole ridge from Beinn na Lice

will be under its shade.

If it does not, I will go down to Hallaig,

to the Sabbath of the dead,

15 where the people are frequenting,

every single generation gone.

They are still in Hallaig,

MacLeans and MacLeods,

all who were there in the time of Mac Gille Chaluim:

20 the dead have been seen alive.

The men lying on the green

at the end of every house that was,

the girls a wood of birches,

straight their backs, bent their heads.

Questions

47 Look at lines 1–12.

    a) Identify any **two** central concerns of the poem which are introduced in these lines.   **2**

    b) By referring to at least **two** examples, analyse how the poet's use of language in these lines develops at least one of these concerns.   **4**

48 Look at lines 13–24. By referring to at least **two** examples, analyse how the poet's use of language in these lines creates a fusion of past and present.   **4**

49 By referring to this poem and to at least one other by MacLean, discuss how he explores the subject of tradition and heritage.   **10**

OR

Text 6 – Poetry

If you choose this text you may not attempt a question on Poetry in Section 2.
Read the extract below and then attempt the following questions.

Nil Nil by Don Paterson

Besides the one setback – the spell of giant-killing
in the Cup (Lochee Violet, then Aberdeen Bon Accord,
the deadlock with Lochee Harp finally broken
by Farquhar's own-goal in the replay)
5   nothing inhibits the fifty-year slide
into Sunday League, big tartan flasks,
open hatchbacks parked squint behind goal-nets,
the half-time satsuma, the dog on the pitch,
then the Boy's Club, sponsored by Skelly Assurance,
10 then Skelly Dry Cleaners, then nobody;
stud-harrowed pitches with one-in-five inclines,
grim fathers and perverts with Old English Sheepdogs
lining the touch, moaning softly.
Now the unrefereed thirty-a-sides,
15 terrified fat boys with callipers minding
four jackets on infinite, notional fields;
ten years of dwindling, half-hearted kickabouts
leaves two little boys – Alastair Watt,
who answers to 'Forty', and wee Horace Madden,
20 so smelly the air seems to quiver above him –
playing desperate two-touch with a bald tennis ball
in the hour before lighting-up time.
Alastair cheats, and goes off with the ball
leaving wee Horace to hack up a stone
25 and dribble it home in the rain;
past the stopped swings, the dead shanty-town
of allotments, the black shell of Skelly Dry Cleaners
and into his cul-de-sac, where, accidentally,
he neatly back-heels it straight into the gutter
30 then tries to swank off like he meant it.

Questions

50 Look at lines 1–13. By referring to at least **two** examples, analyse how the poet's use of language conveys the extent of the club's decline.

4

51 Look at lines 14–22. By referring to at least **two** examples, analyse how the poet's use of language creates a depressing mood in these lines.

4

52 Look at lines 23–30. Analyse how the poet's use of language creates sympathy for 'wee Horace'.

2

53 By referring to this poem and to at least one other poem by Paterson, discuss the importance of time and change in his poetry.

10

[End of Section 1]

A

Section 2 – Critical Essay – 20 marks

Attempt **ONE** question from the following genres – Drama, Prose Fiction, Prose Non-Fiction, Poetry, Film and Television Drama, or Language.

Your answer must be on a different genre from that chosen in Section 1.

You should spend approximately 45 minutes on this Section.

Part A – Drama

Answers to questions on Drama should refer to the text and to such relevant features as characterisation, key scene(s), structure, climax, theme, plot, conflict, setting ...

1   Choose a play which explores one of the following themes: revenge, betrayal, sacrifice.

   Discuss, with reference to appropriate techniques, how the dramatist explores your chosen theme.

2   Choose from a play an important scene which you find amusing or shocking or moving.

   Explain briefly why the scene is important to the play as a whole and discuss, with reference to appropriate techniques, how the dramatist makes the scene amusing or shocking or moving.

3   Choose a play in which a character makes a crucial error.

   Explain what the error is and discuss, with reference to appropriate techniques, to what extent it is important to your understanding of the character's situation in the play as a whole.

Part B – Prose Fiction

Answers to questions on Prose Fiction should refer to the text and to such relevant features as characterisation, setting, language, key incident(s), climax, turning point, plot, structure, narrative technique, theme, ideas, description ...

4   Choose a novel **or** short story which explores the cruelty of human nature.

   Explain, with reference to appropriate techniques, how the writer explores this theme and discuss how the exploration of the theme adds to your appreciation of the text as a whole.

5   Choose a novel **or** short story in which a conflict between a central character and at least one other character is of central importance in the text.

   Explain the circumstances of the conflict and discuss, with reference to appropriate techniques, its importance to your understanding of the text as a whole.

6   Choose a novel **or** short story which ends in a way you find particularly satisfying.

   Briefly describe the ending and, with reference to appropriate techniques, discuss why you find the ending satisfying in terms of your understanding of the text as a whole.

Part C – Prose Non-Fiction

Answers to questions on Prose Non-Fiction should refer to the text and to such relevant features as ideas, use of evidence, stance, style, selection of material, narrative voice …

Non-fiction texts can include travel writing, journalism, autobiography, biography, essays …

7 Choose a non-fiction text in which the writer expresses outrage or shock about an issue which you feel is important.

Discuss, with reference to appropriate techniques, how the writer conveys this emotion.

8 Choose a non-fiction text in which the writer brings one or more than one key incident vividly to life.

Discuss, with reference to appropriate techniques, how the writer achieves this and how it adds to your understanding of the text as a whole.

9 Choose a non-fiction text which, in your opinion, deals with a fundamental truth about human nature.

Discuss, with reference to appropriate techniques, how the writer explores this fundamental truth and to what extent your understanding of it is enhanced.

Part D – Poetry

Answers to questions on Poetry should refer to the text and to such relevant features as word choice, tone, imagery, structure, content, rhythm, rhyme, theme, sound, ideas …

10 Choose a poem which reveals a complex character.

Discuss, with reference to appropriate techniques, how the poet reveals the complexity of the character.

11 Choose a poem in which there is a powerful evocation of place.

Discuss, with reference to appropriate techniques, how the poet presents the place and how this adds to your appreciation of the poem as a whole.

12 Choose a poem in which the poet presents an apparently ordinary situation or event in an extraordinary way.

Discuss, with reference to appropriate techniques, how the poet gives impact and meaning to the apparently ordinary situation or event.

Part E – Film and Television Drama

Answers to questions on Film and Television Drama* should refer to the text and to such relevant features as use of camera, key sequence, characterisation, mise-en-scène, editing, music/sound, special effects, plot, dialogue ...

13 Choose a film **or** television drama in which a particular atmosphere is an important feature.

Explain, with reference to appropriate techniques, how the film or programme makers create this atmosphere and discuss how it contributes to your appreciation of the text as a whole.

14 Choose a film **or** television drama which explores a crisis in a relationship or the break-up of a family.

Discuss, with reference to appropriate techniques, how the film or programme makers' exploration of the crisis or break-up contributes to your understanding of character and/or theme.

15 Choose from a film **or** television drama an important sequence in which a tense mood is created.

Explain, with reference to appropriate techniques, how the film or programme makers create the tension in the sequence and discuss the importance of the sequence to the text as a whole.

* 'Television drama' includes a single play, a series or a serial.

Part F – Language

Answers to questions on Language should refer to the text and to such relevant features as register, accent, dialect, slang, jargon, vocabulary, tone, abbreviation ...

16 Choose the language of live broadcasting, such as live news coverage, sports commentaries, award ceremonies.

Identify specific examples of this language and discuss, with reference to appropriate features of language, to what extent it is effective in communicating the event to its target audience.

17 Choose some of the rhetorical devices which underpin success in speechmaking.

Identify specific examples of this language and discuss, with reference to appropriate features of language, the effectiveness of your chosen rhetorical devices.

18 Choose aspects of language associated with a particular vocational group such as lawyers, doctors or engineers.

Identify specific examples of this language and discuss, with reference to appropriate features of language, to what extent this shared language contributes to the effectiveness of the group's vocational activities.

[End of Section 2]
[End of question paper]

Higher
English

HODDER
GIBSON
LEARN MORE

Paper 1: Reading for Understanding, Analysis and Evaluation

Duration: 90 minutes

Total marks: 30

Attempt ALL questions.

In the exam you must write your answers clearly in the answer booklet provided and clearly identify the question number you are attempting.

Use **blue** or **black** ink.

The following two passages consider the problems of having too much choice.

Passage 1

Read the passage below and then attempt questions 1–6.

In the first passage, Ben Macinlyre reflects on some experiences on a holiday in Florida.

The Tyranny of Choice

Last week, on holiday in Florida, I went to a supermarket near Fort Myers to buy some breakfast cereal with the children, and suffered the first of a series of choice overdoses. A vast canyon of cereals stretched to the horizon, a universe of flakes, crunchies, puffs and additives, an overflowing cornucopia of baffling breakfast options. The children
5   whooped, and began grabbing at the boxes. A fight broke out over Trix, Froot Loops, Chex, or Cheerios, and then another over the specific variety of Cheerios. The youngest wept bitterly when her heart's desire – some sort of sawdust in teddy bear shapes and radioactive pastels – was flatly rejected by the other two. As the debate raged, I counted 137 separate cereals, and 8 different combinations of variety pack. There are,
10 I subsequently learnt, 275 different sorts of cereal available in the US. I made an executive decision. We would go to a restaurant for breakfast.

'With your pancakes or waffles do you want hash browns, grits, cheese grits, fried potatoes, syrup, maple or walnut, strawberry, cherry or blueberry topping?' said the waitress. 'With the coffee is that whole milk, organic, skimmed milk, half 'n' half, eggs
15 well done, over-medium, over easy, scrambled, poached ...?' 'Er, why don't you choose?' I suggested. She looked scandalised, horrified at this dereliction of the God-given duty to choose. No one had ever not chosen in her restaurant before. It was weird. It was un-American.

But it was the jeans rack, in the outlet store next door, that finally broke me. I wanted some normal blue jeans; what I was offered was relaxed fit, easy fit, slim fit, distressed, traditional
20 cut, stone-washed, acid-washed, zipper, button, low-slung, classic, frayed, boot-leg, drainpipe, turn-up. 'Relaxed, or easy?' asked the saleswoman brightly. 'Neither,' I snarled, and left.

The tyranny of choice is not peculiar to America; it has taken root wherever choice is conflated, quite wrongly, with freedom. Some Eastern European intellectuals in former Communist countries look back nostalgically at a time when so many choices, about food, clothing, housing,
25 were made by others, or strictly limited, giving people time to concentrate on more useful activities, like thinking. Some choice is essential to the patina of life, but too much, according to the latest research, merely promotes anxiety, uncertainty, and even clinical depression.

We have become shackled to the demands of choice. Time, the commodity that should truly be ours to spend freely, is stolen by the years spent pondering what, in the vast, bogus and
30 repetitive menu laid before us, we really want. And built into all these choices is a permanent and inescapable disappointment. When we choose one of the 275 sorts of cereal we inevitably harbour a suspicion that we cannot have chosen the best one. And so we quest, hopelessly, after some ideal thing that the advertisers insist is exactly right for us, just waiting to be chosen.

Even when we believe we have made the right choice, we live in fear of post-payment trauma:
35 people who have bought a new car subsequently enjoy watching advertisements for that car, but avoid information about rival makes.

The psychologist Barry Schwartz, in his book *The Paradox of Choice*, argues that the superabundance of choice has become a crushing burden, as consumers are themselves consumed by the pressure to choose. A society that prizes personal selection as an
40 intrinsic virtue inevitably encourages what Schwartz labels 'maximisers', those people who relentlessly hunt out the best, or best price, from the multiplicity of options, and discourages 'satisficers' (combining satisfaction and sacrifice), who simply go through the possibilities until they find something acceptable. Maximisers are doomed to depression, to channel surf through life in the mistaken belief that there is always something better on the other side; the
45 satisficers make do, and are happier for it.

A plethora of choices can be self-defeating. One might expect that with, say, 57 varieties on offer, more consumers would find contentment more often. Research has shown that the reverse is true. Offer buyers half a dozen types of sausages, and they will probably choose one without difficulty; give them 100 choices, and they are far more likely to buy nothing at all.
50 A single item with a reduced price in a shop window will attract buyers; but put two different items, equally marked down, in the same window, and buyers become uncertain, with a substantial drop in sales.

Weighed down by choice, we postpone a choice of mate, delaying and searching, paralysed by the maximisers' myth of Mr or Miss Right. We ponder and doubt and repeatedly take our life
55 choices back to the vendor, insisting that they are never quite the right fit.

But a revolution is brewing against the tyranny of choice. Internet shopping sets a template of purchases, allowing one to choose, at a click, exactly what was chosen before. Another method of limiting choice is what social scientists now call 'self-binding pre-commitment'. This used to be known as a shopping list. Or we could simply choose not to waste any more
60 time choosing but take the first acceptable thing we come across, and then get on with something more important (i.e. just about anything). As the old proverb goes, 'No choice is also a choice'; it is also a lot less confusing and time-consuming.

On the plane back from Florida the stewardess leant over and with real anguish admitted: 'There is no more chicken or pasta, I'm afraid. Just the beef casserole.'

65 'That's fine,' I reassured her. 'We all have to make satisfices.'

Passage 2

Read the passage below and attempt question 7. While reading, you may wish to make notes on the main ideas and/or highlight key points in the passage.

In the second passage, Tim Lott explores the problem of too much choice.

Choose to Have Less Choice

Once, when I was suffering a fit of depression, I walked into a supermarket to buy a packet of washing powder. Confronted by a shelf full of different possibilities, I stood there for 15 minutes staring at them, then walked out without buying any washing powder at all.

5 I still feel echoes of that sensation of helplessness. If I just want to buy one item but discover that if I buy three of the items I will save myself half the item price, I find myself assailed by choice paralysis.

I hate making consumer choices at the best of times, because I have this uncomfortable suspicion that big companies are trying to gull me out of as much money as possible, using sophisticated techniques designed by people who are smarter than I am.

10 This issue of choice and complexity lies at the heart of the experience of being modern. It penetrates commerce, politics and our personal lives. It may even be connected to the fact that there are higher levels of depression in society than ever before.

Choice oppresses us. Why? Because there are too many choices and they are often too complex for us to be confident that we are making the right one.

15 When you might have 200 potential choices to make of a particular style of camera, it is difficult to feel sure you have chosen the right one – even if you spend an inordinate amount of time trying to make a rational decision. Or you may see the same model two weeks after you've bought it being sold more cheaply. When there was less choice and fewer types of camera, this kind of experience was rare. Our capacity for hindsight has become a means of punishing ourselves.

20 This complexity is not entirely accidental. Modern capitalism solves the dilemma of competition (for the producer) through complexity. To try to choose a mortgage, or a pension, or a computer, requires a tremendous amount of application, so we become relatively easy to gull. Whether it is a power company or a loan company, we struggle to understand tariffs, terms and the small print. Exhausted, we just take a stab and hope for the best, or

25 we succumb to inertia; choose what we have always chosen. Consumers are thrown back on simple cues that are advantageous to the producers, such as brand recognition.

This problem of choice and complexity is ubiquitous. It applies in medicine. If I am ill and asked to make a choice about treatment, I would often rather leave the choice to the doctor, if only because if the wrong choice is made, I am not going to feel nearly so bad about it. I had

30 a prostate cancer scare recently, and I just wanted to be told what to do – not decide whether, say, I should choose an operation that would guarantee impotency in order to stave off a 5% chance of cancer. The burden of choice was too big.

In the personal realm, once, you stayed married for life. Now, if you are in an unhappy marriage you have to decide whether to stay or not. These may be all positive developments,

35 but they come at a cost – the potential for regret.

So how should one react to complexity? Perhaps we should limit choice, not extend it. If you are shopping for food, go to supermarkets that are priced simply with a limited range, such as Aldi and Lidl. Recognise and accept complexity – which means accepting that you can never be sure that you've made the right choice.

40

Above all, don't fall for the old trope of only wanting 'the best'. In his book *The Paradox of Choice*, Barry Schwartz calls such people 'maximisers' – people who are never happy, because they have expectations that can never be met, since in a world of complexity and unlimited choice there is always a better option. Be a

45 'satisficer' instead – people who are happy to say 'that's good enough', or 'it'll do'. As a consumer, and in life generally, it's a pretty good formula. It'll do, anyway.

Questions

MARKS

1 Read lines 1– 21.

   a) Using your own words as far as possible, summarise the key points of the writer's experiences in Florida.

   4

   b) By referring to **at least two** examples, analyse how the writer's language creates a light-hearted tone in this part of the passage.

   4

2 Read lines 22–27. Using your own words as far as possible, explain why 'Some Eastern European intellectuals in former Communist countries look back nostalgically'.

   2

3 Read lines 28–36.

   a) Using your own words as far as possible, explain what the writer believes is wrong with having too much choice.

   2

   b) By referring to **at least two** examples, analyse how the writer's word choice conveys his negative attitude to choice.

   4

4 Read lines 37–45. Using your own words as far as possible, explain the difference between a 'maximiser' and a 'satisficer'.

   2

5 Read lines 46–55. Using your own words as far as possible, explain why having too much choice can be 'self-defeating'.

   3

6 Read lines 56–65. Evaluate the effectiveness of these lines as a conclusion to the passage as a whole. In your answer you should refer to ideas **and** to language.

   4

Question on both passages

7 Look at both passages. Both writers express their views about choice.

   Identify **three** key areas on which they agree. You should support the points by referring to important ideas in both passages.

   You may answer this question in continuous prose or in a series of developed bullet points.

   5

[End of question paper]

Paper 2: Critical Reading

Duration: 90 minutes

Total marks: 40

Section 1 – Scottish Text – 20 marks

Read an extract from a Scottish text you have previously studied and attempt the questions.

Choose ONE text from either

Part A – Drama   Pages 40–44

or

Part B – Prose   Pages 44–50

or

Part C – Poetry   Pages 51–58

Attempt ALL questions for your chosen text.

Section 2 – Critical Essay – 20 marks

Attempt ONE question from the following genres – Drama, Prose Fiction, Prose Non-Fiction, Poetry, Film and Television Drama, or Language.

Your answer must be on a different genre from that chosen in Section 1.

You should spend approximately 45 minutes on each Section.

In the exam you must write your answers clearly in the answer booklet provided and clearly identify the question number you are attempting.

Use **blue** or **black** ink.

Section 1 – Scottish Text – 20 marks

Choose ONE text from Drama, Prose or Poetry.

Read the text extract carefully and then attempt ALL the questions for your chosen text.

You should spend about 45 minutes on this Section.

Part A – Scottish Text – Drama

Text 1 – Drama

If you choose this text you may not attempt a question on Drama in Section 2.

Read the extract below and then attempt the following questions.

The Slab Boys by John Byrne

In this extract, which is from near the end of the play, Lucille surprises everyone with her choice of partner for the Staffie.

(*Enter* LUCILLE *dressed for home*)

LUCILLE: Burton's Corner ... quarter to ... okay?

(PHIL *and* SPANKY *look towards each other*)

ALAN: Yeh ... right, Lucille.

5 PHIL & SPANKY: (*Together*) Eh??

LUCILLE: Are you sure you can get your Dad's M.G.?

ALAN: No problem ...

LUCILLE: And put some cream on that pimple ... I swear it's twice the size it was this morning.

10 ALAN: For God's sake ...

LUCILLE: (*To* PHIL) Sorry ... I couldn't've went through with it even if I had said, yeh ... you can see that, can't you? I mean to say ... look at him ... he's a skelf.

PHIL: You're looking at a skelf that's branching out, doll ...

LUCILLE: Aw, go to hell. And if I was you I wouldn't go home via Storey Street ...
15 that's where Bernadette's boyfriend's got his jew-jipsey parlour. He eats smouts like you for his breakfast! (*To* ALAN) If you're not there on the dot I'm going in by myself so be warned! (*Exits*)

ALAN: Listen, Heck ...

HECTOR: (*Bravely*) Don't worry about it, Alan ... I'm taking Willie Curry on my ticket.
20 Well, you guys, I better shoot off ... Willie's giving us a lift down the road. You can keep that fitch if you find it, anybody.

(*Changes into overcoat*)

SPANKY: Heh ... hold on, Hector ... you can't go just like that. What about that money we gave you?

25 HECTOR: Aw, yeh ... a quid, wasn't it? No ... I'll just hold onto that, if youse don't mind. Help towards a skin graft for my ear and the down payment on a nylon overall like Jimmy Robertson's got. 'Night all ... (*Exits*)

	SPANKY:	The cocky little …
		(HECTOR *re-enters*)
30	HECTOR:	And I'll be expecting some smart grinding from this department in the future. No palming me off with sub-standard shades, Farrell. Oh … sorry to hear you lost your job, Phil. Not to worry … you'll not find much difference now you're 'officially' out of work. (*Takes Parker pen from* PHIL*'s pocket and hands it to* ALAN) See
35		youse at the Staffie. (*Exits*)
	ALAN:	I better push off, too … heavy night ahead. (*Changes for home*)
	SPANKY:	Christ, I even let him into the secrets of gum making … what happens? He strolls off into the sunset with the dame hanging from his top lip. Yeh, I think you better push off, Archie … go on … beat it.
40		(ALAN *crosses to door … stops*)
	ALAN:	(*To* PHIL) There's always next year, you know …
	PHIL:	You heard … beat it!
	ALAN:	Fine. I was going to say 'sorry' but I can see you're doing a pretty good job of that on your own. See you at the Dance … buy you a
45		small beer perhaps? And I'll be seeing you on Monday … Sparky … so take it easy on the floor … watch out nobody steps on your fingers … there's quite a bit of grinding to get through … That cabinet out there's an embarrassment …

Questions

MARKS

1 Look at lines 1–17. Explain what is revealed in these lines about Lucille's character.

2

2 Look at lines 19–35. By referring to at least **two** examples in these lines, explain how Hector's new-found confidence is made clear.

4

3 Look at lines 43–48. By referring to at least **two** examples in these lines, analyse how Alan's attitude to Phil and Spanky is conveyed.

4

4 By referring to this extract and to elsewhere in the play, discuss the role of Lucille **or** Hector in *The Slab Boys.*

10

OR

Text 2 – Drama

If you choose this text you may not attempt a question on Drama in Section 2.

Read the extract on the next page and then attempt the following questions.

The Cheviot, the Stag and the Black, Black Oil by John McGrath

In this extract Andy McChuckemup, a property developer, outlines his vision for the future of the Highlands.

ANDY: The motel – as I see it – is the thing of the future. That's how we see it, myself and the Board of Directors, and one or two of your local Councillors – come on now, these are the best men money can buy. So – picture it, if yous will, right there at the top of the glen, beautiful vista – The Crammem Inn, High Rise
5 Motorcroft – all finished in natural, washable, plastic granitette. Right next door, the 'Frying Scotsman' All Night Chipperama – with a wee ethnic bit, Fingal's Caff – serving seaweed-suppers-in-the-basket, and draught Drambuie. And to cater for the younger set, yous've got your Grouse-a-go-go. I mean, people very soon won't want your bed and breakfasts, they want everything laid on, they'll be
10 wanting their entertainment and that, and wes've got the know-how to do it and wes have got the money to do it. So – picture it, if yous will – a drive-in clachan on every hill-top where formerly there was hee-haw but scenery.

Enter LORD VAT OF GLENLIVET, *a mad young laird.*

LORD VAT: Get off my land – these are my mountains.

15 ANDY: Who are you, Jimmy?

LORD VAT: Lord Vat of Glenlivet. I come from an ancient Scotch family and I represent the true spirit of the Highlands.

ANDY: Andy McChuckemup of Crammem Inn Investments Ltd., Govan, pleased for to make your acquaintance Your Worship. Excuse me, is this your fields?

20 LORD VAT: You're invading my privacy.

ANDY: Excuse me, me and wor company's got plans to develop this backward area into a paradise for all the family – improve it, you know, fair enough, eh?

LORD VAT: Look here, I've spent an awful lot of money to keep this place private and peaceful. I don't want hordes of common people trampling all over the
25 heather, disturbing the birds.

ANDY: Oh no, we weren't planning to do it for nothing, an' that – there'll be plenty in it for you …

LORD VAT: No amount of money could compensate for the disruption of the couthie way of life that has gone on here uninterrupted for yonks. Your Bantu – I mean your
30 Highlander – is a dignified sort of chap, conservative to the core. From time immemorial, they have proved excellent servants – the gels in the kitchen, your sherpa – I mean your stalker – marvellously sure-footed on the hills, your ghillie-wallah, tugging the forelock, doing up your flies – you won't find people like that anywhere else in the world. I wouldn't part with all this even if you
35 were to offer me half a million pounds.

ANDY: A-ha. How does six hundred thousand suit you?

LORD VAT: My family have lived here for over a century; 800,000.

ANDY: You're getting a slice of the action, Your Honour – 650,000.

LORD VAT: I have my tenants to think of. Where will they go? 750,000.

40 ANDY: We'll be needing a few lasses for staff and that … 700,000 including the stately home.

LORD VAT: You're a hard man, Mr. Chuckemup.

ANDY: Cash.

LORD VAT: Done [*Shake.*]

Questions

MARKS

5 Look at lines 1–12.

    a) Explain what impression is created of Andy's character in these lines.   2

    b) By referring to at least **two** specific details of his plan, analyse how each one is made to sound comical.   4

6 Look at lines 14–44. Analyse how the dramatist makes Lord Vat a figure of fun to the audience in these lines.   4

7 By referring to this extract and to elsewhere in the play, discuss McGrath's use of caricatures **and/or** stereotypes in *The Cheviot, the Stag and the Black, Black Oil.*   10

OR

Text 3 – Drama

If you choose this text you may not attempt a question on Drama in Section 2.

Read the extract below and then attempt the following questions.

Men Should Weep by Ena Lamont Stewart

In this extract from near beginning of the play, Lily questions some of Maggie's assumptions.

LILY:	Dae you think *you're* happy?
MAGGIE:	Aye! I'm happy!
LILY:	In this midden?
MAGGIE:	Ye canna help havin a midden o a hoose when there's kids under yer feet a day. I dae the best I can.
LILY:	I ken ye do. I'd gie it up as hopeless. Nae hot water. Nae place tae dry the weans' clothes … nae money. If John wad gie hissel a shake …
MAGGIE:	You leave John alane! He does his best for us.
LILY:	No much o a best. O.K. O.K. Keep yer wig on! Ye're that touchy ye'd think ye wis jist new merriet. I believe you still love him!
MAGGIE:	Aye. I still love John. And whit's more, he loves me.
LILY:	Ye ought to get yer photies took and send them tae the Sunday papers! 'Twenty-five years merriet and I still love ma husband. Is this a record?'
MAGGIE:	I'm sorry for you, Lily. I'm right sorry for you.
LILY:	We're quits then.
MAGGIE:	Servin dirty hulkin brutes o men in a Coocaddens pub.
LILY:	Livin in a slum and slavin efter a useless man an his greetin weans.
MAGGIE:	They're *my* weans! I'm workin for ma ain.
LILY:	I'm *paid* for my work.

Line numbers in margin: 5, 10, 15, 20

MAGGIE:	So'm I! No in wages … I'm paid wi love. (*Pause*) And when did you last have a man's airms roon ye?	
LILY:	*Men*! I'm wantin nae man's airms roon me. They're a dirty beasts.	
MAGGIE:	Lily, yer mind's twisted. You canna see a man as a man. Ye've got them a lumped thegither. Ye're daft!	
LILY:	You're *saft*! You think yer man's wonderful and yer weans is a angels. Look at Jenny …	
MAGGIE:	(*Instantly on the defensive*) There's naethin wrang wi Jenny!	
LILY:	No yet.	

25 appears beside the third speech (MAGGIE).

Questions

8 Look at lines 1–16.

    a) Explain at least **two** aspects of Maggie's character which are revealed in these lines. **4**

    b) Explain **one** important aspect of Lily's character which is revealed in these lines. **2**

9 Look at lines 17–29. By referring to at least **two** examples, analyse how these lines are structured in such a way as to provide a lively dramatic exchange between Maggie and Lily. **4**

10 By referring to this extract and to elsewhere in the play, discuss to what extent men in the play are presented as weak. **10**

Part B – Scottish Text – Prose

Text 1 – Prose

If you choose this text you may not attempt a question on Prose in Section 2.
Read the extract below and then attempt the following questions.

The Crater by Iain Crichton Smith

They screamed again, in the sound of the shells, and they seemed to hear an answer. They heard what seemed to be a bubbling. 'Are you there?' said Robert, bending down and listening. 'Can you get over here?' They could hear splashing and deep below them breathing, frantic breathing as if someone was frightened
5 to death. 'It's all right,' he said, 'if you come over here, I'll send my rifle down. You two hang on to me,' he said to the others. He was terrified. That depth, that green depth. Was it Morrison down there, after all? He hadn't spoken. The splashings came closer. The voice was like an animal's repeating endlessly a mixture of curses and prayers. Robert hung over the edge of the crater. 'For
10 Christ's sake don't let me go,' he said to the other two. It wasn't right that a man should die in green slime.

He hung over the rim holding his rifle down. He felt it being caught, as if there was a great fish at the end of a line. He felt it moving. And the others hung at his heels,

like a chain. The moon shone suddenly out between two clouds and in that moment
15 he saw it, a body covered with greenish slime, an obscene mermaid, hanging on to
his rifle while the two eyes, white in the green face, shone upward and the mouth,
gritted, tried not to let the blood through. It was a monster of the deep, it was a
sight so terrible that he nearly fell. He was about to say, 'It's no good, he's dying,'
but something prevented him from saying it, if he said it then he would never forget
20 it. He knew that. The hands clung to the rifle below in the slime. The others pulled
behind him. 'For Christ's sake hang on to the rifle,' he said to the monster below.
'Don't let go.' And it seemed to be emerging from the deep, setting its feet against
the side of the crater, all green, all mottled, like a disease. It climbed as if up a
mountainside in the stench. It hung there against the wall.

25 'Hold on,' he said. 'Hold on.' His whole body was concentrated. This man must
not fall down again into that lake. The death would be too terrible. The face was
coming over the side of the crater, the teeth gritted, blood at the mouth. It hung
there for a long moment and then the three of them had got him over the side.
He felt like cheering, standing up in the light of No Man's Land and cheering.
30 Sergeant Smith was kneeling down beside the body, his ear to the heart. It was
like a body which might have come from space, green and illuminated and slimy.
And over it poured the merciless moonlight.

'Come on,' he said to the other two. And at that moment Sergeant Smith said,
'He's dead.'

Questions

11 Look at lines 1–11. By referring to at least **two** examples, analyse how the
writer uses sound to intensify the atmosphere.

4

12 Look at lines 12–24. By referring to at least **two** examples, analyse how the
language used creates a nightmarish atmosphere.

4

13 By referring to lines 25–34, discuss what the sentence 'And over it poured the
merciless moonlight' (line 32) contributes to the conclusion of the extract.

2

14 By referring to this extract and to at least one other story by Crichton Smith,
discuss how he creates tension his stories.

10

OR

Text 2 – Prose

If you choose this text you may not attempt a question on Prose in Section 2.

Read the extract on the next page and then attempt the following questions.

B

The Bright Spade by George Mackay Brown

One night there was a meeting in the ale-house. All the men of the island were there. They took counsel together about the impending famine. That same morning the old man of Cornquoy who lived alone, the fiddler, had been found dead in his chair, after he had been missed for a week. They broke down his
5   door. The young dog was gnawing at the corpse's thigh. Jacob got his fiddle the night he shrouded him, though he knew nothing about music. The fiddle, once a sweet brimming shell, hung at Jacob's wall like a shrivelled chrysalis. The old fiddler was as light as a bird to handle. He needed a narrow grave.

'The meal and the meat are done in the island,' said Harald of Ness at the meeting.
10 'I've eaten nothing myself but a handful of cold potatoes every day for the past week. My suggestion is this, that seven of the strongest men among us cross between the hills to the shore and get a large supply of limpets and dulse from the rocks at low tide.'

The men agreed that it would be necessary to do that.

The seven men chosen set off at dawn the next day. They were Harald of Ness, Adam
15 of Skarataing, Ezekiel of the Burn, Thomas and Philip of Graystones, Simon the blacksmith, and Walter of Muce. That same morning the worst blizzard of winter descended, great swirling blankets of snow out of the east. Tinkers saw the seven men between the hills going towards the shore, like a troop of spectres. They were never seen again until their bodies were dug from the drifts a week later.

20 For the second time that winter Jacob laid seven men together in the kirkyard. This time he would accept no payment at all for his services – 'for,' said he, 'it seems I have done better this winter than anyone else in the island …'.

In March Francis Halcrow the coughing sailor who had been with John Paul Jones in the American Wars died at Braebuster. Jacob buried him for his set of
25 Nantucket harpoons.

And then men brought out ploughs, harness, harrows. The implements were dull and rusty after the hard winter. Jacob's spade, on the other hand, was thin and bright with much employment. 'God grant,' he said to the spade, putting it away in his shed, 'that I won't be needing you again till after the shearing and the
30 lobster fishing and the harvest.'

Questions

15 Look at lines 1–8. By referring to at least **two** examples, analyse how the writer creates a detached, purely factual tone in these lines.

    4

16 Look at lines 9–13. Explain what impression the narrator creates of Harald of Ness as a person in these lines.

    2

17 Look at lines 20–30. By referring to at least **two** aspects of character, explain what is revealed about Jacob as a person.

    4

18 By referring to this extract and to at least one other story by Mackay Brown, discuss his use of symbolism in his stories.

    10

OR

Text 3 – Prose

If you choose this text you may not attempt a question on Prose in Section 2.

Read the extract below and then attempt the following questions.

The Trick Is To Keep Breathing by Janice Galloway

In this extract Joy meets 'Dr Three'.

The doctor is over an hour late. An entirely different man to Dr Two. But questions involve risk and I don't want to look picky. I follow him down the sea-coloured corridor to a room with no pictures and all the curtains closed. It smells like dog in the rain. Dr Three doesn't waste any time.

5	DR THREE	[Sitting] Well?

Leather elbow patches on his horrible jacket glint in the gloom. Behind the specs his eyes are all iris.

	PATIENT	[Mesmerised] Well what? I thought you would start.
10	DR THREE	Start what? Start what? You asked to see me. You are the one who knows what this is about.
	PATIENT	I've been here nearly a week.
	DR THREE	Yes. So what can I do for you?
	PATIENT	[Confused. Has forgotten and is trying to remember.] Treatment. I want to know about treatment.
15	DR THREE	[Leans back with an ominous creak] I don't know what sort of thing you expected. There's no set procedure for these things. You ask to see one of us when you feel you need to. So. Any other questions?
	PATIENT	I have to think. [Silence]
	DR THREE	Well?
20	PATIENT	[Nothing. Eyes filling up.]
	DR THREE	[Draws a long breath through the nose, leaning back on the chair] How long have you been here did you say?
	PATIENT	Nearly a week. I haven't seen anyone.
25	DR THREE	[Sighing] I suppose you want a pass. [Silence] To go home for the weekend? You should be going home on pass. Getting out of here and facing up to things on the outside. You can go out on pass any time you like, all right?
	PATIENT	No. I don't understand any of this.
	DR THREE	I don't know what that's supposed to mean.
	PATIENT	It's too fast. You're rushing me.
30	DR THREE	All right. Take your time. [Silence] Right then. Good day.

He taps the bundle of papers on his desk, then folds his arms. The interview is finished. PATIENT stands thinking maybe this is some kind of therapy.

	DR THREE	The interview is over. [Opens a drawer. The stack of papers flake dangerously. He pretends not to notice.]

Questions

19 Look at lines 1–7. Explain how the writer establishes an unwelcoming atmosphere in these lines.

2

20 Look at lines 8–23. By referring to at least **two** examples, analyse how the exchange between the Patient and Dr Three in these lines highlights the lack of communication between them.

4

21 Look at lines 24–34. By referring to at least **two** examples, explain how the Doctor's uncaring approach is made clear.

4

22 By referring to the extract and elsewhere in the novel, discuss how *The Trick Is To Keep Breathing* explores the way the individual is treated within the mental health system.

10

OR

Text 4 – Prose

If you choose this text you may not attempt a question on Prose in Section 2.

Read the extract below and then attempt the following questions.

Sunset Song by Lewis Grassic Gibbon

This extract from Part 1 (Ploughing) describes Chris's experiences at Duncairn College.

Every week or so the drawing master, old Mr Kinloch, marched out this class or that to the playground in front of the wolf-beast; and down they'd all get on the chairs they'd brought and try and draw the beast. Right fond of the gentry was Kinloch, if you wore a fine frock and your hair was well brushed and your father

5   well to the fore he'd sit beside you and stroke your arm and speak in a slow sing-song that made everybody laugh behind his back. *Noooooooooooooo, that's not quate raight,* he would flute, *More like the head of one of Chrissie's faaaaaaaather's pigs than a heraaaaaaaaaaaldic animal, I'm afraaaaaaaaaaaaaaaaaid.*

So he loved the gentry, did Mr Kinloch, and God knows he was no exception

10 among the masters there. For the most of them were sons and daughters of poor bit crofters and fishers themselves, up with the gentry they felt safe and unfrightened, far from that woesome pit of brose and bree and sheetless beds in which they had been reared. So right condescending they were with Chris, daughter of a farmer of no account, not that she cared, she was douce and

15 sensible she told herself. And hadn't father said that in the sight of God an honest man was as good as any school-teacher and generally a damned sight better?

But it vexed you a bit all the same that a creature like the Fordyce girl should be cuddled by Mr Kinloch when she'd a face like a broken brose-cap and a voice like a nail on a slate. And but little cuddling her drawing warranted, her father's

20 silver had more to do with it, not that Chris herself could draw like an artist,

Latin and French and Greek and history were the things in which she shone. And the English master set their class an essay on *Deaths of the Great* and her essay was so good that he was forced to read it aloud to all the class, and the Fordyce quean had snickered and sniffed, so mad she was with jealousy.

25 Mr Murgetson was the English master there, not that he was English himself, he came from Argyll and spoke with a funny whine, the Highland whine, and the boys swore he had hair growing up between his toes like a Highland cow, and when they'd see him coming down a corridor they'd push their heads round a corner and cry *Moo!* like a lot of cattle. He'd fly in an awful rage at that, and once
30 when they'd done it he came into the class where Chris was waiting her lesson and he stood and swore, right out and horrible, and gripped a black ruler in his hands and glared round as if he meant to murder a body. And maybe he would if the French teacher, her that was bonny and brave, hadn't come simpering into the room, and then he lowered the ruler and grunted and curled up his lip and said
35 *Eh? Canaille?* and the French teacher she simpered some more and said *May swee.*

So that was the college place at Duncairn, two Chrisses went there each morning, and one was right douce and studious and the other sat back and laughed a canny laugh at the antics of the teachers and minded Blawearie brae and the champ of horses and the smell of dung and her father's brown, grained
40 hands till she was sick to be home again.

Questions

23 Look at lines 1–8. By referring to at least **two** examples, analyse how the writer's use of language in these lines conveys Chris's contempt for Mr Kinloch. **4**

24 By referring to lines 9–35, explain why Chris dislikes the teachers in the College. **4**

25 Look at lines 36–40. Analyse how the writer's use of language in these lines conveys Chris's preference for home. **2**

26 By referring to the extract and to elsewhere in the novel, discuss the way Grassic Gibbon presents Chris as an independent spirit. **10**

OR

Text 5 – Prose

If you choose this text you may not attempt a question on Prose in Section 2.

Read the extract on the next page and then attempt the following questions.

B

The Cone-Gatherers by Robin Jenkins

In this extract from Chapter 1, Duror is secretly watching the cone-gatherers.

Hidden among the spruces at the edge of the ride, near enough to catch the smell of larch off the cones and to be struck by some of those thrown, stood Duror the gamekeeper, in an icy sweat of hatred, with his gun aimed all the time at the feebleminded hunchback grovelling over the rabbit. To pull the
5   trigger, requiring far less force than to break a rabbit's neck, and then to hear simultaneously the clean report of the gun and the last obscene squeal of the killed dwarf would have been for him, he thought, release too, from the noose of disgust and despair drawn, these past few days, so much tighter.

He had waited over an hour there to see them pass. Every minute had been
10 a purgatory of humiliation: it was as if he was in their service, forced to wait upon them as upon his masters. Yet he hated and despised them far more powerfully than ever he had liked and respected Sir Colin and Lady Runcie-Campbell. While waiting, he had imagined them in the darkness missing their footing in the tall tree and coming crashing down through the sea of branches
15 to lie dead on the ground. So passionate had been his visualising of that scene, he seemed himself to be standing on the floor of a fantastic sea, with an owl and a herd of roe-deer flitting by quiet as fish, while the yellow ferns and bronzen brackens at his feet gleamed like seaweed, and the spruce trees swayed above him like submarine monsters.

20 He could have named, item by item, leaf and fruit and branch, the overspreading tree of revulsion in him; but he could not tell the force which made it grow, any more than he could have explained the life in himself, or in the dying rabbit, or in any of the trees about him.

This wood had always been his stronghold and sanctuary; there were many
25 places secret to him where he had been able to fortify his sanity and hope. But now the wood was invaded and defiled; its cleansing and reviving virtues were gone. Into it had crept this hunchback, himself one of nature's freaks, whose abject acceptance of nature, like the whining prostrations of a heathen in front of an idol, had made acceptance no longer possible for Duror himself. He was humpbacked,
30 with one shoulder higher than the other; he had no neck, and on the misshapen lump of his body sat a face so beautiful and guileless as to be a diabolical joke.

Questions

27 Look at lines 1–8. Analyse how the language in these lines conveys Duror's loathing for Calum.   2

28 Look at lines 9–19. By referring to at least **two** examples, analyse how the writer makes the reader aware of Duror's disturbed state of mind.   4

29 Look at lines 20–31. By referring to at least **two** examples, analyse how the imagery in these lines gives insight into Duror's feelings.   4

30 By referring to this extract and to elsewhere in the novel, discuss the conflict between Duror and the cone-gatherers.   10

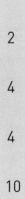

Part C – Scottish Text – Poetry

Text 1 – Poetry

If you choose this text you may not attempt a question on Poetry in Section 2.
Read the extract below and then attempt the following questions.

To a Mouse by Robert Burns

Thy wee-bit housie, too, in ruin!
It's silly wa's the win's are strewin!
An' naething, now, to big a new ane,
O' foggage green!
5 An' bleak December's winds ensuin,
Baith snell an' keen!

Thou saw the fields laid bare an' waste,
An' weary winter comin fast,
An' cozie here, beneath the blast,
10 Thou thought to dwell,
Till crash! the cruel coulter past
Out thro' thy cell.

That wee-bit heap o' leaves an' stibble,
Has cost thee mony a weary nibble!
15 Now thou's turn'd out, for a' thy trouble,
But house or hald,
To thole the winter's sleety dribble,
An' cranreuch cauld!

But Mousie, thou art no thy lane,
20 In proving foresight may be vain;
The best-laid schemes o' mice an' men
Gang aft agley,
An' lea'e us nought but grief an' pain,
For promis'd joy!

25 Still thou art blest, compar'd wi' me!
The present only toucheth thee:
But och! I backward cast my e'e,

B

On prospects drear!

An' forward, tho' I canna see,

30   I guess an' fear!

Questions

31 Look at lines 1–6. Analyse how the poet's language creates sympathy for the mouse's situation in these lines.

2

32 Look at lines 7–18. By referring to at least **two** examples, analyse how the poet's language in these lines conveys the impact of man on the mouse's way of life.

4

33 Look at lines 19–30. By referring to at least **two** examples, analyse how the poet's language in these lines creates an effective mood on which to conclude the poem.

4

34 By referring to this poem and to at least one other by Burns, discuss his use of at least one specific verse form.

10

OR

Text 2 – Poetry

If you choose this text you may not attempt a question on Poetry in Section 2.
Read the poem below and then attempt the following questions.

Anne Hathaway by Carol Ann Duffy

The bed we loved in was a spinning world

of forests, castles, torchlight, clifftops, seas

where he would dive for pearls. My lover's words

were shooting stars which fell to earth as kisses

5   on these lips; my body now a softer rhyme

to his, now echo, assonance; his touch

a verb dancing in the centre of a noun.

Some nights, I dreamed he'd written me, the bed

a page beneath his writer's hands. Romance

10   and drama played by touch, by scent, by taste.

In the other bed, the best, our guests dozed on,

dribbling their prose. My living laughing love –

I hold him in the casket of my widow's head

as he held me upon that next best bed.

Questions

35 Look at lines 1–3. ('The bed ... pearls.') Analyse how the poet's language in the first sentence establishes the speaker's passion.

2

36 Look at lines 3–10. ('My lover's words ... taste.') By referring to at least **two** examples, analyse how the poet uses references to writing and literature in these lines to convey the speaker's feelings.

4

37 Look at lines 11–14. By referring to at least **two** examples, analyse how these lines bring the poem to an effective conclusion.

4

38 By referring to this poem and to at least one other by Duffy, discuss how she explores the theme of love.

10

OR

Text 3 – Poetry

If you choose this text you may not attempt a question on Poetry in Section 2.

Read the extract below and then attempt the following questions.

Last Supper by Liz Lochhead

Already she was imagining it done with, this feast, and

exactly

what kind of leftover hash she'd make of it

among friends, when it was just

5 The Girls, when those three met again.

What very good soup

she could render from the bones,

then something substantial, something extra

tasty if not elegant.

10 Yes, there they'd be, cackling around the cauldron,

spitting out the gristlier bits

of his giblets;

gnawing on the knucklebone of some

intricate irony;

15 getting grave and dainty at the

petit-gout mouthfuls of reported speech.

'That's rich!' they'd splutter,

munching the lies, fat and sizzling as sausages.

Then they'd sink back

20   gorged on truth

and their own savage integrity,

sleek on it all, preening

like corbies, their bright eyes blinking

satisfied

25   till somebody would get hungry

and go hunting again.

Questions

39   Look at lines 1–9. Analyse how the poet develops the metaphor of 'this feast'.   2

40   Look at lines 10–16. By referring to at least **two** examples, analyse how the poet uses sound in these lines to create a negative impression of 'The Girls'.   4

41   Look at lines 17–26. By referring to at least **two** examples, analyse how the poet's language in these lines describes the people at the supper.   4

42   By referring to this poem and to at least one other by Lochhead, discuss her use of humour and/or wordplay to explore serious issues.   10

OR

Text 4 – Poetry

If you choose this text you may not attempt a question on Poetry in Section 2.

Read the poem below and then attempt the following questions.

Basking shark by Norman MacCaig

To stub an oar on a rock where none should be,

To have it rise with a slounge out of the sea

Is a thing that happened once (too often) to me.

But not too often – though enough. I count as gain

5   That I once met, on a sea tin-tacked with rain,

That roomsized monster with a matchbox brain.

He displaced more than water. He shoggled me

Centuries back – this decadent townee

Shook on a wrong branch of his family tree.

10   Swish up the dirt and, when it settles, a spring

Is all the clearer. I saw me, in one fling,

Emerging from the slime of everything.

So who's the monster? The thought made me grow pale

For twenty seconds while, sail after sail,

15   The tall fin slid away and then the tail.

Questions

43 Look at lines 1–6. By referring to at least **two** examples, analyse how the poet's language in these lines conveys the strangeness of what happened.

4

44 Look at lines 7–9. By referring to at least **two** examples, analyse how the poet's language in these lines creates a light-hearted tone.

4

45 By referring to lines 10–12, explain what prompts the poet to ask 'So who's the monster?' (line 13).

2

46 By referring to this poem and to at least one other by MacCaig, discuss how satisfying you find the way he ends his poems.

10

B

OR

Text 5 – Poetry

If you choose this text you may not attempt a question on Poetry in Section 2.

Read the poem below and then attempt the following questions.

I gave you immortality by Sorley MacLean

I gave you immortality
and what did you give me?
Only the sharp
arrows of your beauty,
5   a harsh onset
and piercing sorrow,
bitterness of spirit
and a sore gleam of glory.

If I gave you immortality
10 you gave it to me;
you put an edge on my spirit
and radiance in my song.
And though you spoiled
my understanding of the conflict,
15 yet, were I to see you again,
I should accept more and the whole of it.

Were I, after oblivion of my trouble,
to see before me
on the plain of the Land of Youth
20 the gracious form of your beauty,
I should prefer it there,
although my weakness would return,
and to peace of spirit
again to be wounded.

25 O yellow-haired, lovely girl,

  you tore my strength

  and inclined my course

  from its aim:

  but, if I reach my place,

30 the high wood of the men of song,

  you are the fire of my lyric –

  you made a poet of me through sorrow.

  I raised this pillar

  on the shifting mountain of time,

35 but it is a memorial-stone

  that will be heeded till the Deluge,

  and, though you will be married to another

  and ignorant of my struggle,

  your glory is my poetry

40 after the slow rotting of your beauty.

Questions

47 Look at lines 1–16. By referring to at least **two** examples, analyse how the poet's language in these lines conveys the speaker's feelings towards the person he is addressing.

4

48 Look at lines 17–24. Analyse how the poet's language in these lines creates a mood of regret.

2

49 Look at lines 25–40. By referring to at least **two** examples, analyse how the poet's language in these lines conveys what he feels he has gained from the relationship.

4

50 By referring to this poem and to at least one other poem by MacLean, discuss the emotional intensity of his poetry.

10

OR

Text 6 – Poetry

If you choose this text you may not attempt a question on Poetry in Section 2.

Read the poem on the next page and then attempt the following questions.

Two Trees by Don Paterson

One morning, Don Miguel got out of bed
with one idea rooted in his head:
to graft his orange to his lemon tree.
It took him the whole day to work them free,
5   lay open their sides, and lash them tight.
For twelve months, from the shame or from the fright
they put forth nothing; but one day there appeared
two lights in the dark leaves. Over the years
the limbs would get themselves so tangled up
10 each bough looked like it gave a double crop,
and not one kid in the village didn't know
the magic tree in Miguel's patio.

The man who bought the house had had no dream
so who can say what dark malicious whim
15 led him to take his axe and split the bole
along its fused seam, then dig two holes.
And no, they did not die from solitude;
nor did their branches bear a sterile fruit;
nor did their unhealed flanks weep every spring
20 for those four yards that lost them everything,
as each strained on its shackled root to face
the other's empty, intricate embrace.
They were trees, and trees don't weep or ache or shout.
And trees are all this poem is about.

Questions

MARKS

51 Look at lines 1–12. By referring to at least **two** examples, analyse how the poet makes these lines sound like the start of a simple folk tale or parable.   4

52 Explain how lines 13–16 act as a link or turning point in the poem as a whole.   2

53 Look at lines 17–24. By referring to at least **two** examples, analyse how the poet undermines the idea that the poem is a parable or a tale with a message.   4

54 By referring to this poem and to at least one other by Paterson, discuss his use of symbolism to explore important themes.   10

[End of Section 1]

Section 2 – Critical Essay – 20 marks

Attempt **ONE** question from the following genres – Drama, Prose Fiction, Prose Non-Fiction, Poetry, Film and Television Drama, or Language.

Your answer must be on a different genre from that chosen in Section 1.

You should spend approximately 45 minutes on this Section.

Part A – Drama

> *Answers to questions on Drama should refer to the text and to such relevant features as characterisation, key scene(s), structure, climax, theme, plot, conflict, setting ...*

1   Choose a play in which a central character's behaviour is at times irrational or unstable or obsessive.

   Describe the nature of the character's behaviour and discuss, with reference to appropriate techniques, how this behaviour affects your understanding of the character in the play as a whole.

2   Choose a play which explores one of the following ideas: the power of love; the nature of heroism; the impact of self-delusion; the burden of responsibility.

   Discuss, with reference to appropriate techniques, how the dramatist explores the idea.

3   Choose from a play a scene which causes you to see a character in a new light.

   Explain, with reference to appropriate techniques, how the scene causes this and discuss how important it is to your understanding of the character in the play as a whole.

Part B – Prose Fiction

> *Answers to questions on Prose Fiction should refer to the text and to such relevant features as characterisation, setting, language, key incident(s), climax, turning point, plot, structure, narrative technique, theme, ideas, description ...*

4   Choose a novel **or** short story in which a central character's behaviour is at times unwise or foolish or misguided.

   Explain, with reference to appropriate techniques, how the character's behaviour is made apparent and discuss how this adds to your understanding of the text as a whole.

5   Choose a novel **or** short story that explores a theme of social or political or moral importance.

   With reference to appropriate techniques, explain how the writer explores this theme and discuss why its exploration adds to your appreciation of the text as a whole.

6   Choose a novel **or** short story in which symbolism plays an important part.

   Discuss, with reference to appropriate techniques, how the writer's use of symbolism is important to your understanding of the text as a whole.

Part C – Prose Non-Fiction

Answers to questions on Prose Non-Fiction should refer to the text and to such relevant features as ideas, use of evidence, stance, style, selection of material, narrative voice ...

Non-fiction texts can include travel writing, journalism, autobiography, biography, essays ...

7 Choose a non-fiction text which presents difficult or challenging ideas in an accessible way.

Explain briefly what is difficult or challenging about the writer's ideas and discuss, with reference to appropriate techniques, how she or he presents them in an accessible way.

8 Choose a non-fiction text which you find to be inspirational or moving.

Explain, with reference to appropriate techniques, how the writer evokes this response and discuss why you find the text inspirational or moving.

9 Choose a non-fiction text which is structured in a particularly effective way.

Discuss, with reference to appropriate techniques, how the structure enhances your understanding of the text as a whole.

Part D – Poetry

Answers to questions on Poetry should refer to the text and to such relevant features as word choice, tone, imagery, structure, content, rhythm, rhyme, theme, sound, ideas ...

10 Choose a poem in which the prevailing mood is sombre and/or unsettling.

Explain, with reference to appropriate techniques, how the poet creates this mood and how this enhances your understanding of the poem as a whole.

11 Choose a poem which is written in a specific poetic form.

Discuss, with reference to appropriate techniques, how the poet's use of this form contributes to your understanding of the poem as a whole.

12 Choose a poem in which the personality of the speaker or of another character is gradually revealed.

Discuss, with reference to appropriate techniques, how the poet achieves the gradual revelation of the personality.

Part E – Film and Television Drama

Answers to questions on Film and Television Drama* should refer to the text and to such relevant features as use of camera, key sequence, characterisation, mise-en-scène, editing, music/sound, special effects, plot, dialogue ...

13 Choose a film **or** television drama in which the true nature of a central character is gradually revealed to the audience.

Explain, with reference to appropriate techniques, how the film or programme makers present the gradual revelation and discuss how this adds to your appreciation of the text as a whole.

14 Choose a film **or** television drama in which one sequence is crucial to your understanding of an important theme.

Discuss, with reference to appropriate techniques, why the sequence is so important to your understanding of the theme.

15 Choose a film **or** television drama which is set in a particular period of history and explores significant concerns of life at that time.

Discuss, with reference to appropriate techniques, how the film or programme makers present the period and explore significant concerns of life at that time.

* 'Television drama' includes a single play, a series or a serial.

Part F – Language

Answers to questions on Language should refer to the text and to such relevant features as register, accent, dialect, slang, jargon, vocabulary, tone, abbreviation ...

16 Choose the language associated with a particular group in society which shares a professional or leisure activity.

Identify specific examples of this language and discuss, with reference to appropriate features of language, how these examples facilitate communication within the group.

17 Choose some of the ways language is evolving as a result of advances in communication technology.

Identify specific examples of this language and discuss, with reference to appropriate features of language, to what extent these advances are improving or impeding communication.

18 Choose the language of persuasion used in advertising or in politics.

Identify specific examples of this language and discuss, with reference to appropriate features of language, how effective it is in its aim to persuade.

[End of Section 2]

[End of question paper]

Higher
English

Paper 1: Reading for Understanding, Analysis and Evaluation

> **Duration: 90 minutes**
>
> **Total marks: 30**
>
> **Attempt ALL questions.**
>
> In the exam you must write your answers clearly in the answer booklet provided and clearly identify the question number you are attempting.
>
> Use **blue** or **black** ink.

The following two passages consider the place of work in our lives.

Passage 1

Read the passage below and then attempt questions 1–7.

In the first passage, Johann Hari describes two experiments which aimed to change the pattern of working lives.

The Culture of Overwork

The people of Utah, one of the most conservative states in the US, have stumbled across a simple policy that slashes greenhouse gas emissions by 13 percent, saves huge sums of money, improves public services, cuts traffic congestion, and makes 82 per cent of workers happier. It all began in 2008, when the state was facing a budget crisis. One night,
5 the Governor, Jon Huntsman, was staring at the red ink and rough sums when he had an idea. Keeping the state's buildings lit and heated and manned cost a fortune. What if, instead of working 9 to 5, Monday to Friday, the state's employees only came in four days a week, but now from 8 to 6? The state would be getting the same forty hours a week out of its staff – but the costs of maintaining their offices would plummet. The employees would
10 get a three-day weekend, and cut a whole day's worth of tiring, polluting commuting out of their week.

He took the step of requiring it by law for 80 per cent of the state's employees (emergency services and prisons were exempted). At first, there was cautious support among the workforce but as the experiment has rolled on, it has gathered remarkable acclaim. Now,
15 82 per cent of employees applaud the new hours, and hardly anyone wants to go back.

A whole series of unexpected benefits started to emerge. The number of sick days claimed by workers fell by 9 per cent. Air pollution fell, since people were spending 20 per cent less time in their cars. Some 17,000 tonnes of warming gases were kept out of the atmosphere. They have a new slogan in Utah – Thank God It's Thursday.

20 Work is the activity that we spend most of our waking lives engaged in – yet it is too often trapped in an outdated routine. Today, very few of us work in factories, yet we have clung to the habits of the factory with almost religious devotion. Clock in, sit at your terminal, be seen to work, clock out. Is this the best way to make us as productive and creative and happy as we can be? Should we clamber into a steel box every morning to sit in a concrete box all day?

25 Some of the best creative works of recent years – think of Ricky Gervais' TV series *The Office*, for example – have distilled the strange anomie of living like this, constantly monitored, constantly sedentary, constantly staring at a screen. In a wired lap-topped world, far more people could work more effectively from home, in hours of their own choosing, if only their bosses would have confidence in them. They would be better workers, better parents and

30 better people – and we would take a huge number of cars off the road.

But the problem runs deeper than this. Britain now has the longest work hours in the developed world after the US – and in a recession, those of us with jobs scamper ever faster in our hamster-wheels. This is not how the 21st century was meant to turn out. If you look at the economists and thinkers of, say, the 1930s, they assumed that once we had achieved

35 abundance – once humans had all the food and clothes and heat and toys we could use – we would relax and work less. They thought that by now work would barely cover three days as we headed en masse for the beach and the concert-hall.

Instead, the treadmill is whirling ever-faster. This isn't our choice: virtually every study of this issue finds that huge majorities of people say they want to work less and spend more time

40 with their friends, their families and their thoughts. We know it's bad for us. You become 37 per cent more likely to suffer a stroke or heart-attack if you work 60 hours a week – yet one in six of all Brits are doing just that.

We don't stop primarily because we are locked in an arms race with our colleagues. If we relax and become more human, we fall behind the person in the next booth down, who is chasing

45 faster. Work can be one of the richest and most rewarding experiences, but not like this.

In the 1990s, the French government discovered an elegant way out of this, taking the Utah experiment deeper and further. They insisted that everyone work a maximum of 35 paid hours a week. It was a way of saying: in a rich country, life is about more than serving corporations and slogging. Wealth generation and consumerism should be our slaves, not our masters:

50 where they make us happy, we should embrace them; where they make us miserable, we should cast them aside. Enjoy yourself. True wealth lies not only in having enough, but in having the time to enjoy everything and everyone around you.

It was the equivalent of an arms treaty: we all stop, together, now, at the 35 hour mark. The French population became fitter, their relationships were less likely to break down, their

55 children became considerably happier, and voluntary organisations came back to life. But under pressure from corporations enraged that their staff couldn't be made to slog all the time, France has abandoned this extraordinary national experiment. The French people were dismayed: the polls show a majority still support the cap.

From the unlikely pairing of Utah and Paris, a voice is calling. It is telling us that if we leave

60 our offices empty a little more, we can find a happier, healthier alternative lying in the great free spaces beyond.

Passage 2

Read the passage below and attempt question 8. While reading, you may wish to make notes on the main ideas and/or highlight key points in the passage.

In the second passage, Owen Jones argues that work threatens to take up even more of our lives in the future.

Free Us from the Drudgery of Work

Work already consumes too much of our lives: for the next generation, it could consume even more. The state pension age will be bumped up to 66 by 2020; and those lucky young things now joining the world of employment could be waiting into their 70s for a state pension. An inevitable by-product of rising life expectancy perhaps; but surely a gift of progress should be
5   the granting of more healthy years of leisure, not fewer.

We should be aspiring to a more balanced life: a period of contributing to the nation before decades of global sightseeing, babysitting for grandchildren, back-to-back boxsets and quality time with partners. Think of septuagenarians chained to desks, performing brain surgery or stacking shelves, and tell me you don't shudder. Will employers even be willing to
10 take on workers of that vintage?

In any case, we already work too much. Research released by the TUC last week showed that British workers put in unpaid overtime worth £31.5bn last year. Five million toiled an average of 7.7 hours a week for zilch. Ever more employees are working excessive hours, defined as more than 48 a week; 3.4 million workers (excluding the self-employed) now work excessive
15 hours, a jump of 15% since 2010.

This simply cannot be good for us. It's hardly a surprise that 9.9 million days were lost to work-related stress, depression or anxiety in 2014/15, though I suspect many suffer in silence. But it is surely time that can be better spent: hours robbed from watching children grow up, taking up new hobbies, widening cultural horizons, or just catching up with sleep.

20 Should we resign ourselves to a bleak future of work devouring even our old age? Surely we should start planning for a world where we work less, rather than more. At the centre of my vision is a society where our lives no longer revolve around work. Work represents the loss of our autonomy, where we are under the control of bosses and employers, a full one-third of our adult lives is spent in submission to them. The alternative is not laziness: reading a book
25 or playing sport all require effort, but these are things we freely do. As we work less, our lives become our own.

It was once taken for granted that progress and working less would go hand in hand. At the outset of the Great Depression, economists suggested we would be working only 15 hours a week by now; but the average full-time British worker today puts in nearly 28 hours more
30 than that. It was presumed that advances in technology would reduce the need for human labour: actually, it can fuel demand for new types of work: the arrival of the personal computer has led to the creation of more than 1,500 new types of job.

The postwar western world enjoyed near-full employment, but that era has long since passed. Not only are unemployment and inactivity rates higher than they once were, but work
35 has become more precarious, with zero-hours contracts, insecure self-employment and reluctant part-time workers. The trend will surely be towards even more precarious work.

This isn't alarmism. Research suggests that technology could, in the next 20 years, mean the automation of 60% of retail jobs. Because technology is destroying more jobs than it is creating, 11m jobs could go.

40 But threats can be opportunities too. Rather than regarding the march of the robots as an existential threat, why not aim for the automation of the entire economy? Wealth would still be created – albeit by an army of machines – but we would be freed from the drudgery of work.

We have a choice: a society where work becomes ever more dominant even as
45 it becomes ever more precarious, where some work until they drop and others are demonised for being unable to work; or a society where we can realise our full potential in every sense, with more time for leisure, for love, for each other. I choose the latter.

Questions

MARKS

1 Read lines 1–19. Using your own words as far as possible, summarise the key points of what happened in Utah in 2008.

4

2 Read lines 20–24. By referring to **at least two** examples, analyse how the writer's use of language creates a negative impression of work.

4

3 Read lines 25–30. By referring to at least one example, analyse how sentence structure is used to clarify what the writer is saying.

2

4 Read lines 31–45.

a) Using your own words as far as possible, explain the difference between what 'economists and thinkers' predicted in the 1930s and what has actually happened.

4

b) By referring to **at least two** examples of imagery in these lines, analyse how the writer conveys his attitude to modern working practices.

4

5 Read lines 46–52. Using your own words as far as possible, explain the thinking behind what the French government did in the 1990s.

3

6 Read lines 53–58. By referring to at least one example, analyse how sentence structure is used to clarify what the writer is saying.

2

7 Read lines 59–61. Analyse how the writer's use of language creates a positive tone on which to conclude the passage.

2

Question on both passages

8 Look at both passages. Both writers express their views about work.

Identify **three** key areas on which they agree. You should support the points by referring to important ideas in both passages.

You may answer this question in continuous prose or in a series of developed bullet points.

5

[End of question paper]

Paper 2: Critical Reading

Duration: 90 minutes

Total marks: 40

Section 1 – Scottish Text – 20 marks

Read an extract from a Scottish text you have previously studied and attempt the questions.

Choose ONE text from either

Part A – Drama   Pages 70–74

or

Part B – Prose   Pages 74–81

or

Part C – Poetry   Pages 81–89

Attempt ALL questions for your chosen text.

Section 2 – Critical Essay – 20 marks

Attempt ONE question from the following genres – Drama, Prose Fiction, Prose Non-Fiction, Poetry, Film and Television Drama, or Language.

Your answer must be on a different genre from that chosen in Section 1.

You should spend approximately 45 minutes on each Section.

In the exam you must write your answers clearly in the answer booklet provided and clearly identify the question number you are attempting.

Use **blue** or **black** ink.

Section 1 – Scottish Text – 20 marks

Choose ONE text from Drama, Prose or Poetry.

Read the text extract carefully and then attempt ALL the questions for your chosen text.

You should spend about 45 minutes on this Section.

Part A – Scottish Text – Drama

Text 1 – Drama

If you choose this text you may not attempt a question on Drama in Section 2.

Read the extract below and then attempt the following questions.

The Slab Boys by John Byrne

In this extract, from Act Two of the play, Alan intervenes on Hector's behalf.

	HECTOR:	D'you like it, Alan?
	ALAN:	It's … er … (PHIL *threatens to snap pen*) … really gadgey, Heck.
	HECTOR:	Will I go now and ask her? Will I? (*Heads for door*)
5	SPANKY:	(*Cutting him off*) Not just yet, Hector … Remember you've still got to go and see Willie.
	HECTOR:	Yeh, but I can do that after I've asked Lucille …
	PHIL:	No, Spanky's right, kiddo … better go and see Willie first. It's important. Lucille'll not go off the boil. Here, I'll give you my coat to put on … (*Takes off coat*)
10	HECTOR:	What do I want that for? I don't mind doing a bit of swanking now that my clothes are up to date.
	PHIL:	Yeh, but you don't want anybody else to get a preview, do you? Lessen the impact … know what I mean? Get the coat on. (*Forces* HECTOR's *arms into sleeves*)
15	SPANKY:	(*Pulling balaclava helmet from cupboard*) You better put this on and all … it's draughty in Willie's room. (*Pulls helmet over* HECTOR's *head*) Cosy, eh?
	HECTOR:	(*Slightly bamboozled*) Yeh, but will he not think I'm a bit happed up?
20	PHIL:	That's just it. You've been down at Nurse. Influenza verging on pleurisy. She ordered you home but you decided to soldier on. He'll like that. Maybe not give you your … (*Stops*)
	SPANKY:	(*Quickly*) Wireless back.
	HECTOR:	I'm not expecting my wireless back. You know what he's like.
	SPANKY:	Well, you can't just expect it back cos you've got the flu, Heck …
	PHIL:	Triple pneumonia, Spanks.
25	HECTOR:	I'm all mixed up … what've I got again?
	SPANKY:	Triple pneumonia …
	PHIL:	Double rupture …
	HECTOR:	I'll away along then.

SPANKY:	Good man. All the best.
30 PHIL:	Good luck, son … (*They shove* HECTOR *out the door*) You'll need it. (*They hold onto each other laughing*)
ALAN:	Well, I hope you're proud of yourselves … that was a pretty lousy trick to play!
SPANKY:	Oh, was it, by jove?
35 PHIL:	A trick, you cad! Take that! (*Bops* ALAN's *head a smack*)
ALAN:	Hey, watch it! That was sore … Chuckit! Okay, so I'm speaking out of turn but that poor little bastard's gone off to Willie Curry's office thinking that underneath that dustcoat and helmet he really does cut a dash … and he'll probably stop off on the way back to have a word with Lucille … doff the coat and hat and you know what'll happen then … she'll wet herself. Which will probably give you and your crummy friend a big laugh, won't it?
PHIL:	Gosh and All Serene … the Fifth Form at St Dominic's. Listen, Steerforth Minor, if it wasn't for me and Spanks there that 'poor little bastard' wouldn't have any pals. Yeh, that's right. So, we do take the piss … set him up a bit …
ALAN:	More than a bit.

Questions

1 Look at lines 1–31. By making at least **two** references to these lines, explain how the audience is made to feel sorry for Hector.

    4

2 Look at lines 32–35. Analyse how the playwright's use of language in these lines allows Phil and Spanky to make fun of Alan.

    2

3 Look at lines 36–47. By referring to at least **two** examples, analyse how the playwright emphasises the animosity between Alan and Phil.

    4

4 By referring to this extract and to elsewhere in the play, discuss the importance of the conflict between Phil and Alan in exploring at least one theme in the play.

    10

C

OR

Text 2 – Drama

If you choose this text you may not attempt a question on Drama in Section 2.

Read the extract below and then attempt the following questions.

The Cheviot, the Stag and the Black, Black Oil by John McGrath

This extract is from near the beginning of the play.

	OLD MAN:	But for every township that fought back, there were many more that didn't. The landlords had an ally in the heart of the community.
		Fiddle plays: 'The Lord is my Shepherd'. *The company hum quietly as one of the actors is dressed as the* MINISTER *and the* OLD MAN *places his pulpit in position.*
5	MINISTER:	Dearly beloved Brethren, we are gathered here today in the sight of the Lord and in the house of the Lord, to worship the Lord and sing His praises, for He is indeed, the Lord and Shepherd of our souls. Oh you are sheep, sheep who have gone astray, who have wandered from the paths of righteousness and into the tents of iniquity. Oh guilty sinners, turn from your evil ways. How many
10		times and on how many Sabbaths have I warned you from this very pulpit of your wickedness and of the wrath of the Almighty. For I will repay, saith the Lord. The troubles that are visiting you are a judgement from God, and a warning of the final judgement that is to come. Some of you here today are so far from the fold, have so far neglected the dignity of your womanhood, that
15		you have risen up to curse your masters, and violate the laws of the land. I refer of course to the burning of the writs. And everybody here gathered knows to which persons I am referring. There will be no more of this foolishness. Be warned. Unless you repent, you are in great danger of the fire, where there will be much wailing and gnashing of teeth. On that fearful day when God
20		divides the sheep from the goats, every one of us, and particularly those whom I have spoken of today, will have to answer for their flagrant transgression of authority.
		He goes off.
	OLD MAN:	And it worked ...
25	SECOND GIRL:	Everywhere, except in Knockan, Elphin and Coigeach.
	FIRST GIRL	*comes on stage and says, to mounting cheers from the others.*
	FIRST GIRL:	Here the people made a stout resistance, the women disarming about twenty policeman and sheriff-officers, burning the summonses in a heap, and ducking the representatives of the law in a neighbouring pool. (*Big cheer.*) The
30		men formed a second line of defence – (*Groan*) – in case the women should receive any ill-treatment. (*More groans.*) They, however, never put a finger on the officers of the law – all of whom returned home without serving a single summons or evicting a single crofter!
		A big hooch from the Company, the fiddle strikes up and they leap onto the stage
35		*to dance to celebrate this victory, the women leading off.*

5   By referring to lines 1–4, explain how disapproval of the Church is established
     at the start of the extract.

2

6   By referring to at least **two** examples in lines 5–22, analyse how the
     playwright's use of language is designed to sound like that of a stereotypical
     minister.

4

7   By referring to at least **two** examples in lines 24–35, analyse how the
     playwright creates a contrast in mood with what has gone before.

4

8   By referring to this extract and to elsewhere in the play, discuss how the
     playwright uses language and/or speech patterns to satirise characters and/or
     ideas.

10

OR

Text 3 – Drama

If you choose this text you may not attempt a question on Drama in Section 2.

Read the extract below and then attempt the following questions.

Men Should Weep by Ena Lamont Stewart

In this extract from near the end of Act One, Jenny arrives home late.

> *John comes in holding Jenny by the arm. She is about eighteen, made up boldly (for
> the nineteen-thirties): her lipstick is spread over her mouth, her coat and blouse
> undone, her hair tousled.*
>
> JENNY: (*Furious*) Leave me go!
>
> 5   *She shakes herself free and she and John stand glaring at each
>   other. Maggie is watching fearfully.*
>
> JENNY: Makin a bloomin fool o me in front o ma friend!
>
> JOHN: Where hae you been till this time o night?
>
> JENNY: That's nane o your business. I'm grown up noo.
>
> 10 JOHN: Don't you speak to me like that. I asked ye where ye'd been.
>
> JENNY: An I tellt ye! Nane o your damned interferin business.
>
> MAGGIE: Jenny! John!
>
>   *John takes Jenny by the shoulders and shakes her.*
>
> JOHN: Where wis ye? Answer me!
>
> 15 JENNY: At the pickshers.
>
> JOHN: The pickchers comes oot at hauf ten. Where wis ye efter?
>
> JENNY: (*Sullen*) Wi Nessie Tate an a coupla friends.

He lets her go and she flops into a chair, glaring sullenly at him and rubbing her shoulder.

20 JOHN: I don't approve o yon Nessie Tait.

JENNY: That's a peety. I dae.

JOHN: Ye impident little bitch! What I ought tae dae is tak ma belt tae ye.

JENNY: Jist you try it!

JOHN: The next time you come in here at this time o night wi yer paint
25   smeared a ower yer face, I wull! Look at yersel!

He drags her over to a mirror, then propels her, resisting, to the sink, where, holding her head under his arm, he scrubs off her make-up.

JOHN: There! And in the future, you'll let yer hair grow tae the colour
30   God meant it tae be an leave it that wey.

Questions

MARKS

9   Look at lines 1–11. By referring to at least **two** aspects of character, explain what impressions are created of Jenny in these lines.   **3**

10 Look at lines 13–23. By referring to at least **two** features, analyse how a dramatic conflict between John and Jenny is created.   **4**

11 Look at lines 24–30. By referring to at least **two** examples, analyse how dialogue and/or stage directions are used to convey John's anger.   **3**

12 By referring to this extract and to elsewhere in the play, discuss the role of Jenny in *Men Should Weep*.   **10**

Part B – Scottish Text – Prose

Text 1 – Prose

If you choose this text you may not attempt a question on Prose in Section 2.

Read the extract below and then attempt the following questions.

The Painter by Iain Crichton Smith

In this extract the narrator describes the fight between Red Roderick and his father-in-law.

As Red Roderick was drunk perhaps the advantage given him by relative youth was to a certain extent cancelled. There was however no doubt that he wished to kill the old man, so enraged was he, so frustrated by the life that tortured him. As they swung their scythes towards each other ponderously, it looked at
5 first as if they could do little harm, and indeed it was odd to see them, as if each was trying to cut corn. However, after some time – while the face of the old man gradually grew more demoniac in a renewal of his youth – he succeeded at last in cutting his son-in-law's left leg so that he fell to the ground, his wife running towards him like an old hen, her skirts trailing the ground like broken wings.

10 But that was not what I meant to tell since the fight in itself, though unpleasant, was not evil. No, as I stood in the ring with the others, excited and horrified, I saw on the edge of the ring young William with his paint-brush and canvas and easel painting the fight. He was sitting comfortably on a chair which he had taken with him and there was no expression on his face at all but a cold clear

15 intensity which bothered me. It seemed in a strange way as if he were asleep. As the scythes swung to and fro, as the faces of the antagonists became more and more contorted in the fury of battle, as their cheeks were suffused with blood and rage, and their teeth were drawn back in a snarl, he sat there painting the battle, nor at any time did he make any attempt to pull his chair back from the

20 arena where they were engaged.

I cannot explain to you the feelings that seethed through me as I watched him. One feeling was partly admiration that he should be able to concentrate with such intensity that he didn't seem able to notice the danger he was in. The other feeling was one of the most bitter disgust as if I were watching a gaze that

25 had gone beyond the human and which was as indifferent to the outcome as a hawk's might be. You may think I was wrong in what I did next. I deliberately came up behind him and upset the chair so that he fell down head over heels in the middle of a brush-stroke. He turned on me such a gaze of blind fury that I was reminded of a rat which had once leaped at me from a river bank, and he

30 would have struck me but that I pinioned his arms behind his back. I would have beaten him if his mother hadn't come and taken him away, still snarling and weeping tears of rage. In spite of my almost religious fear at that moment, I tore the painting into small pieces and scattered them about the earth. Some people have since said that what I wanted to do was to protect the good name of the

35 village but I must in all honesty say that that was not in my mind when I pushed the chair over. All that was in my mind was fury and disgust that this painter should have watched this fight with such cold concentration that he seemed to think that the fight had been set up for him to paint, much as a house exists or an old wall.

Questions

13 Look at lines 1–9. By referring to at least **two** examples, analyse how the narrator's account creates an ambiguous impression of how serious the fight is.

4

14 Look at lines 10–20. By referring to at least **two** examples, analyse how the writer's language makes clear the contrast between William and the two fighters.

4

15 By referring to lines 21–39, describe in your own words why the narrator is so incensed at William.

2

16 By referring to this extract and to at least one other story by Crichton Smith, discuss the importance of sudden and/or unexpected moments in his stories.

10

OR

Text 2 – Prose

If you choose this text you may not attempt a question on Prose in Section 2.

Read the extract below and then attempt the following questions.

The Eye of the Hurricane by George Mackay Brown

In this extract Captain Stevens tries to convince the narrator to buy him alcohol.

'Now, Barclay, about this cold of mine.'

'Miriam says you haven't got a cold at all,' I said.

'The little bitch,' he said. 'Did she go into your room? She had no right to be disturbing you. I'll speak to her about that. I expect she told you also that I have drinking bouts.'

5   'She did,' I said.

'Well,' he said, 'everybody knows. Can't do a thing about it, Barclay. It's a natural thing, like a storm, you just have to let it blow itself out, keep the ship headed into it. Do you understand that, Barclay?'

'I know nothing about it,' I said.

10   'I thought writers are supposed to understand things,' he said, 'the quirks of human nature. That's what they're for. Don't take hard what I say, Barclay. I like you. I'm very glad you're living in this house. I'm just explaining the situation to you, setting the course through the storm, so that you can take your turn at navigating if the need arises. The best way you can help the voyage, Barclay, is just do what I say. I'm the skipper of this ship. And the first thing I
15   want you to do is open that drawer and you'll see a wallet.'

'No,' I said, and got to my feet.

'There should be four five-pound notes in it. Take one of them out.'

'No,' I said.

'Two bottles of navy rum from Wilson's, as quick as you can.'

20   Charity is no hard-minted currency to be distributed according to whim, a shilling here and a sovereign there – it is the oil and wine that drop uncertainly through the fingers upon the wounds of the world, wherever the roads of pity and suffering cross. It might help this old man, as he said, if I stood close beside him on the bridge till this particular hurricane blew itself out. But I trusted the older wisdom of women. I had made a promise to Miriam.

25   'No,' I said.

'Very well, Mr Barclay,' he said after a pause. 'Let me see. At the moment you are paying me a rent of two pounds a week, I think. As from Monday next you will pay me four pounds a week. In fact, I think you should make arrangements to leave this house before the end of the month. I find you an unsatisfactory tenant. Now get out.'

30   All night, till I fell into a drowse around three o'clock in the morning, I heard him pacing back and fore, back and fore in his room, an ancient mariner in a ship of dark enchantment.

Questions

17 By referring to the whole extract, explain at least **two** methods the Captain uses to convince the narrator to buy him alcohol.

4

18 Look at lines 20–24. By referring to at least **two** examples, analyse how the narrator uses imagery in these lines to explain his views on charity.

4

19 Explain what the last paragraph (lines 30–31) suggests about the narrator's feelings for the Captain.

2

20 By referring to this extract and to at least one other story by Mackay Brown, discuss how he creates confrontations between characters.

10

OR

Text 3 – Prose

If you choose this text you may not attempt a question on Prose in Section 2.

Read the extract below and then attempt the following questions.

The Trick Is To Keep Breathing by Janice Galloway

In this extract Tony takes Joy out for the evening.

There I am in the mirror, inoffensive in a dress with a thick belt to show what remains of the curves. New stockings and slingbacks despite the time of year. Lack of practicality is sexy in women's clothes. The gravel and the crunch of brakes outside makes me stare harder. I try not to hear the different size of shoe
5 thudding on the boards.

Hello? Anybody home?

I see Tony from the top of the stairs, holding up a bottle in white paper, green glass and a foil neck pushing up from the tissue like a clumsy orchid.

Anticipation, he says. Always take it for granted I'm going to win.

10 The lips disappear into his beard and the teeth appear, very white and straight. It's definitely Tony. He tells me I look lovely, a real picture. I want to tell him it's not me but I smile instead. He reaches out his hand and says it again.

You look lovely. You really do.

The car is the wrong colour. It plays Country and Western Music as we ease onto
15 the main road.

She's on form, he says. Should have seen her this afternoon.

The seat creaks with his weight: now we're round the corner, he relaxes.

Called round on the offchance you were home but no such luck. Thought you weren't well? Anyway, she's looking good. Nearly as good as you.

20 He pats my leg.

Expect a treat tonight.

I know we're talking about a dog and try to think of something appropriate to say. In the pause, he sings along with the tape.

When you're in love with a beautiful woman, it's hard

25 He looks sidelong to see my reaction, encouraging me to be cute. He keeps doing it between the sentences.

Maybe after the race we could go somewhere. On the town. Assume you haven't eaten. Could do with some more even if you have. Few more pounds and you'd be a stunner. How are things by the way? I always forget to ask. You never
30 look ill to me so I forget to ask.

Then somebody hangs up when you answer the phone

Just relax and listen to the music. This one's my favourite. Dr Hook. Classic. You don't mind if I run it again. You look great. Should wear a dress more often. Hiding your best assets.

35 He looks over again, his face melting on the double-take.

Christ what did you do to your hands?

I look and see the knuckles bruised and oozy. This is not feminine.

A dopey voice says Oops. I tripped. Silly me.

I tell myself I am with Tony in his car. I tell myself all the way to Glasgow.

Questions

MARKS

21 Look at lines 1–13. By referring to at least **two** aspects of character, explain how Tony is portrayed as an unpleasant character in these lines.

4

22 By referring to lines 14–26, explain how the writer creates an uneasy atmosphere in the car.

2

23 Look at lines 27–39. By referring to at least **two** examples, analyse how aspects of Tony's character are revealed in these lines.

4

24 By referring to this extract and to elsewhere in the novel, discuss Joy's relationships with men.

10

OR

Text 4 – Prose

If you choose this text you may not attempt a question on Prose in Section 2.

Read the extract on the next page and then attempt the following questions.

Sunset Song by Lewis Grassic Gibbon

In this extract from Part III (Seed-time), a disagreement arises at the wedding celebration.

Up at Rob's table an argument rose, Chris hoped that it wasn't religion, she saw Mr Gordon's wee face pecked up to counter Rob. But Rob was just saying what a shame it was that folk should be shamed nowadays to speak Scotch – or they called it Scots if they did, the split-tongued sourocks! Every damned little narrow
5 dowped rat that you met put on the English if he thought he'd impress you – as though Scotch wasn't good enough now, it had words in it that the thin bit scraichs of the English could never come at. And Rob said *You can tell me, man, what's the English for sotter, or greip, or smore, or pleiter, gloaming or glunching or well-kenspeckled? And if you said gloaming was sunset you'd fair be a liar; and*
10 *you're hardly that, Mr Gordon.*

But Gordon was real decent and reasonable, *You can't help it, Rob. If folk are to get on in the world nowadays, away from the ploughshafts and out of the pleiter, they must use the English, orra though it be.* And Chae cried out that was right enough, and God! who could you blame? And a fair bit breeze got up about it all, every
15 soul in the parlour seemed speaking at once; and as aye when they spoke of the thing they agreed that the land was a coarse, coarse life, you'd do better at almost anything else, folks that could send their lads to learn a trade were right wise, no doubt of that, there was nothing on the land but work, work, work, and chave, chave, chave, from the blink of day till the fall of night, no thanks from the
20 soss and sotter, and hardly a living to be made.

Syne Cuddiestoun said that he'd heard of a childe up Laurencekirk way, a banker's son from the town he was, and he'd come to do farming in a scientific way. So he'd said at first, had the childe, but God! by now you could hardly get into the place for the clutter of machines that lay in the yard; and *he* wouldn't
25 store the kiln long. But Chae wouldn't have that, he swore *Damn't, no, the machine's the best friend of man, or it would be so in a socialist state. It's coming and the chaving'll end, you'll see, the machine'll do all the dirty work.* And Long Rob called out that he'd like right well to see the damned machine that would muck you a pigsty even though they all turned socialist to-morrow.

Questions

25 Look at lines 1–10. By referring to at least **two** examples, analyse how the writer conveys the strength of Rob's feelings about language.

4

26 Look at lines 11–20. Explain how the writer conveys in these lines the harshness of life working the land.

2

27 Look at lines 21–29. By referring to at least **two** examples, analyse how the writer's use of language conveys the conflicting views about 'scientific' farming methods.

4

28 By referring to this extract and to elsewhere in the novel, discuss to what extent *Sunset Song* is a celebration of a traditional way of life or an illustration of the inevitability of change.

10

C

Text 5 – Prose

If you choose this text you may not attempt a question on Prose in Section 2.

Read the extract below and then attempt the following questions.

The Cone-Gatherers by Robin Jenkins

In this extract from Chapter 6, Calum witnesses the killing of a deer.

Calum no longer was one of the beaters; he too was a deer hunted by remorseless men. Moaning and gasping, he fled after them, with no hope of saving them from slaughter but with the impulse to share it with them. He could not, however, be so swift or sure of foot. He fell and rose again; he avoided one
5 tree only to collide with another close to it; and all the time he felt, as the deer must have, the indifference of all nature; of the trees, of tall withered stalks of willowherb, of the patches of blue sky, of bushes, of piles of cut scrubwood, of birds lurking in branches, and of the sunlight: presences which might have been expected to help or at least sympathise.

10 The dogs barked fiercely. Duror fired his gun in warning to those waiting in the ride. Neil, seeing his brother rush into the danger, roared to him to come back. All the beaters, except Charlie in the rear, joined in the commotion; the wood resounded with their exultant shouts. Realising this must be the finish or kill, Graham, recuperating on the road, hopped back over the fence into the wood and
15 bellowed loudest of all.

As Duror bawled to his dogs to stop lest they interfere with the shooting, and as the deer hesitated before making the dash across the ride, Calum was quite close to them as, silent, desperate, and heroic, they sprang forward to die or escape. When the guns banged he did not, as Neil had vehemently warned him
20 to do, fall flat on the ground and put his fingers in his ears. Instead, with wails of lament, he dashed on at demented speed and shot out onto the broad green ride to hear a deer screaming and see it, wounded in the breast and forelegs, scrabbling about on its hindquarters. Captain Forgan was feverishly reloading his gun to fire again. Calum saw no one else, not even the lady or Mr. Tulloch,
25 who was standing by himself about twenty yards away.

Screaming in sympathy, heedless of the danger of being shot, Calum flung himself upon the deer, clasped it round the neck, and tried to comfort it. Terrified more than ever, it dragged him about with it in its mortal agony. Its blood came off onto his face and hands.

30 While Captain Forgan, young Roderick, and Lady Runcie-Campbell stood petrified by this sight, Duror followed by his dogs came leaping out of the wood. He seemed to be laughing in some kind of berserk joy. There was a knife in his hand. His mistress shouted to him: what it was she did not know herself, and he never heard. Rushing upon the stricken deer and the frantic hunchback, he
35 threw the latter off with furious force, and then, seizing the former's head with one hand cut its throat savagely with the other. Blood spouted. Lady Runcie-Campbell closed her eyes. Captain Forgan shook his head slightly in some kind of denial. Roderick screamed at Duror. Tulloch had gone running over to Calum.

The deer was dead, but Duror did not rise triumphant; he crouched beside it, on
40   his knees, as if he was mourning over it. His hands were red with blood; in one of
them he still held the knife.

Questions

29   Look at lines 1–9. Analyse how the sentence structure in these lines helps to
convey how Calum is feeling.

2

30   Look at lines 10–29. By referring to at least **two** examples, analyse how the
writer's use of language in these lines creates a sense of 'commotion' (line 12).

4

31   Look at lines 30–41. By referring to at least **two** examples, analyse how the
writer makes the reader aware in these lines of Duror's state of mind.

4

32   By referring to this extract and to elsewhere in the novel, discuss how the
writer presents the character of Calum.

10

Part C – Scottish Text – Poetry

Text 1 – Poetry

If you choose this text you may not attempt a question on Poetry in Section 2.
Read the extract below and then attempt the following questions.

Tam o' Shanter by Robert Burns

In this extract Tam manages to outrun the witches.

As bees bizz out wi' angry fyke,

When plundering herds assail their byke;

As open pussie's mortal foes,

When, pop! she starts before their nose;

5   As eager runs the market-crowd,

When 'Catch the thief!' resounds aloud;

So Maggie runs, the witches follow,

Wi' mony an eldritch skriech and hollo.

Ah, Tam! ah, Tam! thou'll get thy fairin!

10   In hell they'll roast thee like a herrin!

In vain thy Kate awaits thy comin!

Kate soon will be a woefu' woman!

Now, do thy speedy utmost, Meg,

And win the key-stane o' the brig;

15   There at them thou thy tail may toss,

A running stream they dare na cross.

But ere the key-stane she could make,

The fient a tail she had to shake!

For Nannie far before the rest,

20   Hard upon noble Maggie prest,

And flew at Tam wi' furious ettle;

But little wist she Maggie's mettle –

Ae spring brought aff her master hale,

But left behind her ain grey tail:

25   The carlin claught her by the rump,

And left poor Maggie scarce a stump.

Now, wha this tale o' truth shall read,

Ilk man and mother's son, take heed;

Whene'er to drink you are inclin'd,

30   Or cutty-sarks run in your mind,

Think! ye may buy the joys o'er dear –

Remember Tam o' Shanter's mare.

Questions

33 Look at lines 1–8. By referring to at least **two** examples, analyse how the extended simile in these lines creates a vivid picture of what is happening.   4

34 Look at lines 9–26. By referring to at least **two** examples, analyse how Burns makes this part of the poem dramatic.   4

35 Look at lines 27–32. To what extent do you think these lines are meant as a serious warning to the reader?   2

36 Referring to this poem and at least one other poem by Burns, discuss the way his poetry passes judgement on people and/or institutions.   10

OR

Text 2 – Poetry

If you choose this text you may not attempt a question on Poetry in Section 2.
Read the poem below and then attempt the following questions.

Valentine by Carol Ann Duffy

Not a red rose or a satin heart.

I give you an onion.
It is a moon wrapped in brown paper.
It promises light

5   like the careful undressing of love.

Here.
It will blind you with tears
like a lover.
It will make your reflection

10   a wobbling photo of grief.

I am trying to be truthful.

Not a cute card or a kissogram.

I give you an onion.
Its fierce kiss will stay on your lips,

15   possessive and faithful
as we are,
for as long as we are.

Take it.
Its platinum loops shrink to a wedding-ring,

20   if you like.
Lethal.
Its scent will cling to your fingers,
cling to your knife.

C

Questions

37 Look at lines 1–5. By referring to at least **two** examples, analyse how the poet's language in these lines creates a dramatic opening to the poem.

4

38 Look at lines 6–17. By referring to at least **two** examples, analyse how the poet's language in these lines describes love in an unusual way.

4

39 Look at lines 18–23. Analyse how the poet's language in these lines creates an unsettling mood.

2

40 By referring to this poem and to at least one other poem by Duffy, discuss her use of striking imagery and/or word choice.

10

OR

Text 3 – Poetry

If you choose this text you may not attempt a question on Poetry in Section 2.
Read the extract below and then attempt the following questions.

The Bargain by Liz Lochhead

The extract is from the end of the poem.

> We queue in a blue haze of hot fat
> for Danny's Do-Nuts that grit
> our teeth with granules of sugar
> I keep
> 5   losing you and finding you –
> two stalls away you thumb
> through a complete set of manuals for
> primary teachers in the thirties
> I rub my sleeve
> 10   on a dusty Chinese saucer
> till the gilt shows through.
> Oh come on   we promised
> we'd not let our affection for the slightly cracked
> trap us into such expenditure again.
> 15   Oh even if it is a bargain
> we won't buy.

The stallholder says we'll be the death of her

she says   see January

it's been the doldrums the day.

20 And it's packing up time

with the dark coming early

and as cold as the river.

By the bus stop I show you

the beady bag and the maybe rosewood box

25 with the inlaid butterfly and the broken catch.

You've bought a record by the Shangri-las

a pin-stripe waistcoat that needs a stitch

it just won't get   and a book called *Enquire*

Within – Upon Everything.

30 The raw cold gets colder.

There doesn't seem to be a lot to say.

I wish we could either mend things

or learn to throw them away.

Questions

MARKS

41 Look at lines 1–19. By referring to at least **two** examples, analyse how the poet's language in these lines conveys the uneasy atmosphere between the couple.   **4**

42 Look at lines 20–29. By referring to at least **two** examples, analyse how the poet's language in these lines conveys the bleak mood of the speaker.   **4**

43 Look at lines 30–33. Analyse how the poet's language in these lines creates a conclusion you find either optimistic **or** pessimistic.   **2**

44 By referring to this poem and to at least one other poem by Lochhead, discuss how she explores the tension that can arise in relationships.   **10**

C

Text 4 – Poetry

If you choose this text you may not attempt a question on Poetry in Section 2.
Read the poem below and then attempt the following questions.

Assisi by Norman MacCaig

The dwarf with his hands on backwards
sat, slumped like a half-filled sack
on tiny twisted legs from which
sawdust might run,
5   outside the three tiers of churches built
in honour of St Francis, brother
of the poor, talker with birds, over whom
he had the advantage
of not being dead yet.

10   A priest explained
how clever it was of Giotto
to make his frescoes tell stories
that would reveal to the illiterate the goodness
of God and the suffering
15   of His Son. I understood
the explanation and
the cleverness.

A rush of tourists, clucking contentedly,
fluttered after him as he scattered
20   the grain of the Word. It was they who had passed
the ruined temple outside, whose eyes
wept pus, whose back was higher
than his head, whose lopsided mouth
said *Grazie* in a voice as sweet
25   as a child's when she speaks to her mother
or a bird's when it spoke
to St Francis.

Questions

45 Look at lines 1–4. Analyse how the poet's use of sound in these lines enhances the description of the dwarf.

2

46 Look at lines 5–17. By referring to at least **two** examples, analyse how the poet creates an ironic tone in these lines.

4

47 Look at lines 20–27. ('It was they … St Francis.') By referring to at least **two** examples, analyse how the poet's language develops the idea of the dwarf as a 'ruined temple'.

4

48 By referring to this poem and to at least one other by MacCaig, discuss his use of wry humour in his poetry.

10

OR

Text 5 – Poetry

If you choose this text you may not attempt a question on Poetry in Section 2.
Read the poem below and then attempt the following questions.

Shores by Sorley MacLean

If we were in Talisker on the shore

where the great white mouth

opens between two hard jaws,

Rubha nan Clach and the Bioda Ruadh,

5   I would stand beside the sea

renewing love in my spirit

while the ocean was filling

Talisker bay forever:

I would stand there on the bareness of the shore

10   until Prishal bowed his stallion head.

And if we were together

on Calgary shore in Mull,

between Scotland and Tiree,

between the world and eternity,

15   I would stay there till doom

measuring sand, grain by grain,

and in Uist, on the shore of Homhsta

in presence of that wide solitude,

I would wait there forever,

20 for the sea draining drop by drop.

And if I were on the shore of Moidart

with you, for whom my care is new,

I would put up in a synthesis of love for you

the ocean and the sand, drop and grain.

25 And if we were on Mol Stenscholl Staffin

when the unhappy surging sea dragged

the boulders and threw them over us,

I would build the rampart wall

against an alien eternity grinding (its teeth).

Questions

MARKS

49 Look at lines 1–10. By referring to at least **two** examples, analyse how the poet's language in these lines conveys the power of natural features.

4

50 Look at lines 11–20. Analyse how the poet's language conveys the speaker's commitment to the person he is addressing.

2

51 Look at lines 21–29. By referring to ideas **and/or** language, evaluate these lines as a conclusion to the poem as a whole.

4

52 By referring to this poem and to at least one other by MacLean, discuss the importance of landscape in his poetry.

10

OR

Text 6 – Poetry

If you choose this text you may not attempt a question on Poetry in Section 2.
Read the poem below and then attempt the following questions.

The Thread by Don Paterson

Jamie made his landing in the world

so hard he ploughed straight back into the earth.

They caught him by the thread of his one breath

and pulled him up. They don't know how it held.

5   And so today I thank what higher will

brought us to here, to you and me and Russ,

the great twin-engined swaying wingspan of us

roaring down the back of Kirrie Hill

and your two-year-old lungs somehow out-revving

10   every engine in the universe.

All that trouble just to turn up dead

was all I thought that long week. Now the thread

is holding all of us: look at our tiny house,

son, the white dot of your mother waving.

Questions

MARKS

53   Look at lines 1–4. Analyse how the poet's use of imagery in these lines conveys his feelings about Jamie at the time of his birth.

2

54   Look at lines 5–10. By referring to at least **two** examples, analyse how the poet's language in these lines conveys his feelings now.

4

55   Look at lines 12–14. ('Now the thread ... waving.') By referring to at least **two** examples, evaluate the effectiveness of this sentence as a conclusion to the poem as a whole.

4

56   By referring to this poem and to at least one other by Paterson, discuss his use of different verse forms to explore important themes.

10

[End of Section 1]

Section 2 – Critical Essay – 20 marks

Attempt **ONE** question from the following genres – Drama, Prose Fiction, Prose Non-Fiction, Poetry, Film and Television Drama, or Language.

Your answer must be on a different genre from that chosen in Section 1.

You should spend approximately 45 minutes on this Section.

Part A – Drama

Answers to questions on Drama should refer to the text and to such relevant features as characterisation, key scene(s), structure, climax, theme, plot, conflict, setting ...

1   Choose a play in which a central character experiences rejection or isolation or loneliness.

Discuss, with reference to appropriate techniques, how the dramatist makes you aware of the character's situation and how this adds to your understanding of character and/or theme in the play as a whole.

2   Choose a play in which the opening scene establishes important elements of theme and/or character.

Explain, with reference to appropriate techniques, how these elements are established in the opening scene and go on to discuss how this contributes to your understanding of the central concern(s) of the play as a whole.

3   Choose a play in which the setting in time and/or place is an important feature.

With reference to appropriate techniques, explain how the dramatist presents the setting and go on to discuss why this is important to your understanding of the play as a whole.

Part B – Prose Fiction

Answers to questions on Prose Fiction should refer to the text and to such relevant features as characterisation, setting, language, key incident(s), climax, turning point, plot, structure, narrative technique, theme, ideas, description ...

4   Choose a novel **or** short story in which a particular mood is dominant.

With reference to appropriate techniques, explain how the writer creates this mood and discuss how the mood contributes to your understanding of character and/or theme in the text as a whole.

5   Choose a novel **or** short story which explores one of the following ideas: loss, futility, failure.

With reference to appropriate techniques, explain how the writer explores this idea and discuss how its exploration adds to your appreciation of the text as a whole.

6 Choose a novel **or** short story in which a central character's hopes or ambitions are thwarted by the behaviour of others and/or by circumstances beyond his or her control.

With reference to appropriate techniques, explain how the writer presents the character's situation and discuss how the character's reaction influences your understanding of character and/or theme in the text as a whole.

Part C – Prose Non-Fiction

Answers to questions on Prose Non-Fiction should refer to the text and to such relevant features as ideas, use of evidence, stance, style, selection of material, narrative voice ...

Non-fiction texts can include travel writing, journalism, autobiography, biography, essays ...

7 Choose a non-fiction text in which you feel the style of writing is a key factor in developing a persuasive argument.

Discuss, with reference to appropriate techniques, how the writer's presentation of the argument is made persuasive.

8 Choose a non-fiction text in which the writer presents the life of an individual in a positive light.

Discuss, with reference to appropriate techniques, how the writer creates this impression of the individual.

9 Choose a non-fiction text in which the writer describes an experience which is frightening or amusing or educational.

Discuss, with reference to appropriate techniques, how the writer conveys that aspect of the experience and how it enhances your appreciation of the text as a whole.

Part D – Poetry

Answers to questions on Poetry should refer to the text and to such relevant features as word choice, tone, imagery, structure, content, rhythm, rhyme, theme, sound, ideas ...

10 Choose a poem in which the use of contrast is important in developing the central concern(s).

Discuss, with reference to appropriate techniques, the poet's use of contrast and show why it is important in developing the central concern(s) of the poem.

11 Choose a poem which explores aspects of human relationships.

Discuss, with reference to appropriate techniques, how the poet explores the subject.

12 Choose a poem whose closing lines you find particularly effective as a conclusion.

Discuss, with reference to appropriate techniques, why you find the closing lines an effective conclusion to the poem as a whole.

Part E – Film and Television Drama

Answers to questions on Film and Television Drama* should refer to the text and to such relevant features as use of camera, key sequence, characterisation, mise-en-scène, editing, music/sound, special effects, plot, dialogue ...

13 Choose a film **or** television drama which focuses on a rivalry or a friendship between two characters.

   Discuss, with reference to appropriate techniques, how the film or programme makers present the characters and discuss how the rivalry or friendship contributes to your understanding of the text.

14 Choose a film **or** television drama which deals with violence but does not glorify it.

   Discuss, with reference to appropriate techniques, how the film or programme makers explore violence in this way.

15 Choose a film **or** television drama in which the opening sequence successfully establishes key features of the text such as setting, mood, genre, character, theme.

   Explain, with reference to appropriate techniques, how the film or programme makers achieve this success and discuss the importance of the sequence to your appreciation of the text as a whole.

* 'Television drama' includes a single play, a series or a serial.

Part F – Language

Answers to questions on Language should refer to the text and to such relevant features as register, accent, dialect, slang, jargon, vocabulary, tone, abbreviation ...

16 Choose some of the ways language differs across generations.

   Identify specific examples of this difference in language and discuss, with reference to appropriate features of language, to what extent this is advantageous to those involved.

17 Choose the technical language associated with a sport, a craft, a profession or one of the arts.

   Identify specific examples of this language and discuss, with reference to appropriate features of language, to what extent you feel such language leads to clearer communication.

18 Choose the language of advertising aimed at promoting goods or entertainment or campaigns or causes.

   Identify specific examples of this language and discuss, with reference to appropriate features of language, how successful the advertising is.

[End of Section 2]

[End of question paper]

Higher
English

Practice Paper A

Paper 1: Reading for Understanding, Analysis and Evaluation

Passage 1

Question	Expected response	Max. mark	Additional guidance
1	Candidates must use their own words. No marks for straight lifts from the passage. 2 marks may be awarded for detailed/insightful comment. 1 mark for more basic comment. (Marks may be awarded 2 or 1+1.)	2	Possible answers include: ■ human life is always given priority over animal life ■ we will go to any lengths to preserve human life regardless of the impact on the animal world ■ we treat animals in captivity with contempt ■ we respond violently when a captive animal poses a threat, despite the fact that it is only obeying instinct.
2	For full marks there should be comments on at least two examples. 2 marks may be awarded for detailed/insightful comment plus quotation/reference. 1 mark for more basic comment plus quotation/reference. 0 marks for quotation/reference alone. (Marks may be awarded 2+2, 2+1+1 or 1+1+1+1.)	4	Possible answers include: ■ exclamatory tone of 'What a travesty is a zoo' suggests contempt ■ 'travesty' suggests perversion, corruption ■ question 'How can it still exist …' suggests disbelief that it does still exist ■ 'legacy' suggests a relic, something left over ■ 'gentlemen collectors and capricious kings' suggests zoos belong in a bygone age of upper-class dilettantes, detached from ordinary life ■ 'animated taxidermy' – dark humour in the idea that the animals are as good as dead and merely brought to life artificially for our entertainment ■ 'exposed' suggests thrown open against his will, at the mercy of the onlookers ■ 'gawping crowds' suggests stupid, mindless, prepared to stare at anything ■ structure of 'Stand up, bend down, turn around' replicates the simple, limited, repetitive movement of the captive bear ■ 'quite mad' shows deep sympathy for the result of the bear's treatment in the zoo.

Question			Expected response	Max. mark	Additional guidance
3	a)		Candidates must use their own words. No marks for straight lifts from the passage. 2 marks may be awarded for detailed/insightful comment. 1 mark for more basic comment. (Marks may be awarded 2 or 1+1.)	2	Possible answers include: ■ elephants, which were once housed in very restricted space and denied the ability to move in a natural way, are no longer kept in the zoo ■ lions are no longer confined in cages but are now kept in an area which makes an attempt to replicate their natural environment.
	b)		2 marks may be awarded for detailed/insightful comment plus quotation/reference. 1 mark for more basic comment plus quotation/reference. 0 marks for quotation/reference alone. (Marks may be awarded 2 or 1+1.)	2	Possible answers include: ■ 'Oh, but ...' at the start of defenders' claim sounds a little bit insincere ■ 'lavish' suggests it is a little bit overdone, extravagant ■ 'illusion' suggests it is a deception, a piece of trickery ■ use of inverted commas at 'Land of the Lions' suggests disapproval of the term, implying 'so-called', that it's a bit pompous ■ 'mocked-up' suggests artificial, rather cheap ■ 'little (high street)' is rather dismissive, reductive ■ use of inverted commas at 'authentic' casts doubt on the zoo's claim ■ 'movie set' suggests contrived, designed to appear as something it is not ■ the use of 'really' in the concluding question suggests strongly that the writer thinks it is not the case.
4			For full marks there should be comments on at least two examples. 2 marks may be awarded for detailed/insightful comment plus quotation/reference. 1 mark for more basic comment plus quotation/reference. 0 marks for quotation/reference alone. (Marks may be awarded 2+2, 2+1+1 or 1+1+1+1.)	4	Possible answers include: ■ 'theocratic' suggests religious zeal, a blinkered outlook ■ 'purist' suggests intolerance if any deviation from one point of view ■ 'cadre' suggests a closed, almost secretive group, well-organised, dedicated to a single cause ■ 'activists' has a hint of militancy ■ list of 'who compare ... more inclined ... who argue' suggests a substantial number of extreme points of view ■ exaggeration of 'compare farming to the Holocaust' suggests how ridiculous some of their beliefs can be

Question			Expected response	Max. mark	Additional guidance
					▪ extreme comparison ('donkey sanctuaries in Syria … suffering children') suggests how outrageous some of their beliefs can be
					▪ simplicity of the sentence 'For these people …' – statement; colon; statement – imitates their dogmatic way of thinking
					▪ 'fringe' suggests they are not part of mainstream belief, are out on the edge.
5			2 marks may be awarded for detailed/insightful comment. 1 mark for more basic comment. (Marks may be awarded 2 or 1+1.)	3	Possible answers include: ▪ she uses her own experience of going to SeaWorld as an example: she admits she was wrong to expect an innocent, enjoyable experience – it was in fact very disturbing to see the way the orcas were treated ▪ she references the documentary *Blackfish* as a telling example of how exposure of the way orcas are treated at SeaWorld had a major influence on public attitudes ▪ she argues that falling attendance at SeaWorld in response to the film is evidence that public opinion is changing (for the better) ▪ she uses emotional language such as 'turn off half your brain', 'perversion of their nature', 'psychotic' in her descriptions of the orcas at SeaWorld to influence the reader to disapprove of their treatment.
6			Candidates must use their own words. No marks for straight lifts from the passage. 1 mark for each point from the 'Additional guidance' column.	5	Possible answers include: ▪ just as humanity has become more advanced/sophisticated, so too has our attitude to animal life ▪ some activities which were once considered acceptable are now disapproved of ▪ there is genuine outrage at egregious examples of cruelty/wanton killing of animals for fun … ▪ … although big game hunting thrives for economic reasons ▪ despite zoos' commendable efforts at conservation work … ▪ … they still take an irresponsible attitude to animals for which they no longer have a use ▪ they continue to keep captive and exploit animals which have a strong appeal to the public ▪ zoos are, to an extent, driven by the need to make money.

Question			Expected response	Max. mark	Additional guidance
7			2 marks may be awarded for detailed/insightful comment (plus quotation/reference if appropriate). 1 mark for more basic comment (plus quotation/reference if appropriate). 0 marks for quotation/reference alone. (Marks may be awarded 2+1 or 1+1+1.)	3	Possible answers include: ■ scathing tone of 'melancholy mammal museums' sums up her strong disapproval of zoos ■ she offers a simple solution (documentaries on TV) as if there is nothing very difficult about it – and the use of colloquial 'kids' emphasises the simplicity of it ■ short blunt sentence 'The species scale is tipping' provides assertive, unambiguous statement that change is coming ■ the imagery of 'scales' links back to 'scales of moral worth' in second paragraph, rounding off the passage ■ reference to Costa Rica is perhaps surprising since it is a relatively poor country, not often used as an example of enlightened thinking ■ question at end is a direct challenge to the reader, almost defying anyone to contradict her.

Question on both passages

Question			Expected response	Max. mark	Additional guidance
8			Candidates may use bullet points in this final question, or write a number of linked statements. Evidence from the passage may include quotations, but these should be supported by explanations. The approach to marking is shown in the 'Additional guidance' column. Key areas of agreement are shown in the grid on the next page. Other answers are possible.	5	The mark for this question should reflect the quality of response in two areas: ■ identification of the key areas of agreement in attitude/ideas ■ the level of detail given in support. The following guidelines should be used: ■ **5 marks** – identification of three key areas of agreement with insightful use of supporting evidence ■ **4 marks** – identification of three key areas of agreement with appropriate use of supporting evidence ■ **3 marks** – identification of three key areas of agreement ■ **2 marks** – identification of two key areas of agreement ■ **1 mark** – identification of one key area of agreement ■ **0 marks** – failure to identify one key area of agreement and/or misunderstanding of task. **NB** A candidate who identifies only two key areas of agreement may be awarded up to a maximum of 4 marks, as follows: ■ 2 marks for identification of two key areas of agreement

Question	Expected response	Max. mark	Additional guidance
			plus either ■ a further 1 mark for appropriate use of supporting evidence to a total of 3 marks **or** ■ a further 2 marks for detailed/insightful use of supporting evidence to a total of 4 marks. A candidate who identifies only one key area of agreement may be awarded up to a maximum of 2 marks, as follows: ■ 1 mark for identification of one key area of agreement ■ a further 1 mark for use of supporting evidence to a total of 2 marks.

Area of agreement		Passage 1	Passage 2
1	moral objection to zoos	an affront to civilised society to treat animals as exhibits for our entertainment	no excuse for confining animals for 'our fleeting distraction and amusement'
2	natural behaviour is inhibited by zoos	freedom of movement is limited	animals are denied the ability to behave the way they would in the wild
3	physical harm caused by zoos	animals killed to protect humans; the arthritic elephants at London Zoo	over-eating; injury from fire, from ingestion of foreign bodies
4	psychological harm caused by zoos	effect of repetitive actions, the bear in Colchester Zoo, the orcas in SeaWorld	incessant pacing, boredom, neurosis, stress
5	changing public attitudes	some progress over the years in our acceptance of mistreatment of animals	public is now more aware of animals' needs
6	interest in zoos waning	attendance at SeaWorld has declined; orca shows have been discontinued	attendances, once in the millions, now going down
7	the financial imperative	the safari business in Africa, the exploitation of 'charismatic megafauna' for income	marine parks part of a billion-dollar industry

Paper 2: Critical Reading

Section 1 – Scottish Text – 20 marks

NB The final question (for 10 marks) on each text should be marked using the general instructions below. Text-specific guidance for each final question is given at the relevant point.

Up to 2 marks can be achieved for identifying elements of commonality as identified in the question.

A further 2 marks can be achieved for reference to the extract given.

6 additional marks can be achieved for discussion of similar references to at least one other part of the text (or to another short story or poem by the writer).

In practice this means:

- 2 marks for identification of **commonality**, e.g. theme, characterisation, use of imagery, setting, or any other key element.

From the **extract**:

- 2 marks for detailed/insightful comment plus quotation/reference
- 1 mark for more basic comment plus quotation/reference
- 0 marks for quotation/reference alone

From at least one **other part of the text** (or one other poem or short story):

- as above for up to 6 marks.

Text 1 – Drama – *The Slab Boys* by John Byrne

Question			Expected response	Max. mark	Additional guidance
1			2 marks may be awarded for detailed/insightful comment plus quotation/reference. 1 mark for more basic comment plus quotation/reference. 0 marks for quotation/reference alone. (Marks may be awarded 1+1.)	2	Possible answers include: ■ nearly everything he says is a question, suggesting he has a right to know everything, can probe into every aspect of their lives ■ the 'Ha' at the start suggests a kind of triumphant 'got you at last' tone ■ use of surnames only ('McCann ... Farrell') suggests he is treating them as inferiors ■ 'C'mon ...' suggests demanding more information, not prepared to settle for vagueness ■ 'The what?' – insisting that Phil reveal in detail what was (allegedly) wrong with him.
2			2 marks may be awarded for detailed/insightful comment plus quotation/reference. 1 mark for more basic comment plus quotation/reference.	4	Possible answers include: ■ 'Nurse to have a look at you' is a reasonably caring suggestion that he could have consulted the nurse, but Phil pretends to take it literally, as if the nurse would be 'looking at' him during a bout of diarrhoea

Question			Expected response	Max. mark	Additional guidance
			0 marks for quotation/reference alone. (Marks may be awarded 2+2, 2+1+1 or 1+1+1+1.)		■ 'You wouldn't get much done down there' refers to not getting much company business done, but Phil turns it into a lavatorial joke, suggesting that he did in fact get 'a lot done' ■ 'fighting the Japanese with dysentery' means they were suffering from dysentery while they were fighting, but Spanky pretends to take it as using dysentery as a weapon, and asks with assumed naivety how they fired it.
3			2 marks may be awarded for detailed/insightful comment plus quotation/reference. 1 mark for more basic comment plus quotation/reference. 0 marks for quotation/reference alone. (Marks may be awarded 2+2, 2+1+1 or 1+1+1+1.)	4	Possible answers include: ■ 'damned cheek' suggests he sees them as insubordinate, insolent ■ 'silly duck's arse haircuts' suggests he finds their hairstyles stupid, probably uses the slang term with some distaste ■ 'that bloody contraption' suggests he disapproves of the radio, sees no value in it ■ 'that racket' suggests he has a low opinion of the music, sees it only as noise ■ 'this gadget' suggests he sees the radio as trivial, a mere contraption ■ 'you bunch' suggests he has no respect for them, just a group like a little gang, not committed to the company ethic ■ 'lounging about' suggests he sees them as lazy, not dedicated to their work.
4			Candidates can answer in bullet points in this final question, or write a number of linked statements. Marks for this question should be allocated following the guidelines given at the start of these Marking Instructions. See page 100.	10	Possible references include: ■ 'typical' ex-Army: disciplinarian, follow-orders-without-question approach ■ puffed up, self-important, has created a self-mythology around his exploits in Burma ■ despairs of and criticises younger generation, their attitude, their music, their clothes ■ sycophantic towards Alan ■ fondness for clichés ('pull your socks up', 'toe the line') and for his own linguistic creations ('faster than you can say Axminster broadloom') ■ dull, straight-laced: Phil and Spanky's patter usually goes over his head, he misses the double entendres, knows Phil and Spanky are making fun of him but doesn't know how ■ but not all bad: surprises audience at end by supporting Phil against Barton (and for having kept secret about Jimmy Robertson).

Text 2 – Drama – *The Cheviot, the Stag and the Black, Black Oil* by John McGrath

Question			Expected response	Max. mark	Additional guidance
5			2 marks may be awarded for detailed/insightful comment plus quotation/reference. 1 mark for more basic comment plus quotation/reference. 0 marks for quotation/reference alone. (Marks may be awarded 2+2, 2+1+1 or 1+1+1+1.)	4	Possible answers include: ■ the 'quiet' song will establish a peaceful, calm atmosphere ■ 'It begins, I suppose' sounds like a natural speaking voice, not assertive, almost diffident ■ 'and all that' is very colloquial ■ 'in a bit of a mess' is very understated, not being dramatic ■ light humour in the response of the singer to information about Gaelic and the plaid ■ 'So …' is very conversational ■ the visually amusing appearance of the cottage ■ two girls singing in Gaelic – unthreatening, pleasing ■ 'making it all seem fine' suggests there was no panic, no unrest ■ 'invented … introduced' – underplaying the severe impact of the Cheviot ■ 'not too pleased about it' is something of an understatement in the light of what actually happened.

6			2 marks may be awarded for detailed/insightful comment plus quotation/reference.
			1 mark for more basic comment plus quotation/reference.
			0 marks for quotation/reference alone.
			For full marks both the Women and the Young Highlander should be covered but not necessarily in equal measure.
			(Marks may be awarded 2+2, 2+1+1 or 1+1+1+1.)
				4	Possible answers include:
					■ The Women are unconcerned, don't complain, shown by:
					  ■ the dismissive 'blethers' which suggests idle talk, not to be taken seriously
					  ■ the defence of the Countess as having been 'kind' to them
					  ■ the First Woman sees no problem with the Countess living the high life ('Why wouldn't she be?')
					  ■ she invalidates the YH's criticism of misuse of rent by claiming he never pays any
					  ■ she is not interested in YH's news about 150 soldiers; ignores it and tells him (or the other woman?) to get on with the work.

Question			Expected response	Max. mark	Additional guidance
					<ul><li>The YH criticises the Countess, is full of complaints, is agitated about idea of soldiers, shown by:<ul><li>his sneering remark about the Countess being an absentee ('away in England')</li><li>his obvious antipathy at 'fancy palaces and feasts for Kings and fine French wines' – sees her as living in luxury (while they have to scrape a living)</li><li>his accusing her of doing so at their expense ('it's our rent she's spending')</li><li>his sense of accumulating grievance in structure of 'If it's not bad weather … it's mildew … and last year it was both together … And now they're talking about …'.</li></ul></li></ul>
7			2 marks may be awarded for detailed/insightful comment plus quotation/reference. 1 mark for more basic comment plus quotation/reference. 0 marks for quotation/reference alone. (Marks may be awarded 1+1.)	2	Possible answers include:<ul><li>the apparently innocuous 'You might find a good use for this' when he hands her the bucket, is actually inviting her to throw the urine at Sellar and Loch, the approaching representatives of authority</li><li>the tongue-in-cheek use (and repetition) of 'gentlemen' to describe two notoriously cruel and heartless characters.</li></ul>
8			Candidates can answer in bullet points in this final question, or write a number of linked statements. Marks for this question should be allocated following the guidelines given at the start of these Marking Instructions. See page 100.	10	Possible references include:<ul><li>the ceilidh format</li><li>the use of the oversized pop-up book as scenery</li><li>audience participation (e.g. in the 'Walla Walla Wooskie' section)</li><li>the use of amusing caricatures and stereotypes</li><li>the irreverent, tongue-in-cheek presentation of historical figures (e.g. Queen Victoria, Harriet Beecher Stowe, Duke of Sutherland)</li><li>the unashamedly didactic political agenda</li><li>reciting/quoting detailed statistics (e.g. about population decline)</li><li>musical extravaganzas such as Texas Jim's square dance.</li></ul>

Text 3 – Drama – *Men Should Weep* by Ena Lamont Stewart

Question			Expected response	Max. mark	Additional guidance
9	a)		2 marks may be awarded for detailed/insightful comment plus quotation/reference. 1 mark for more basic comment plus quotation/reference. 0 marks for quotation/reference alone. (Marks may be awarded 2+2, 2+1+1 or 1+1+1+1.)	4	Possible answers include: ■ 'I dinna ken … at a' expresses her bewilderment, anguish, sadness ■ 'Slavin an worryin … an naethin but heartbreak' conveys the lack of fulfilment she feels despite all the effort ■ 'a yer days' emphasises the lifelong commitment ■ her response to Alec's comforting gesture (*'she looks up at him gratefully, lovingly, and lays his hand to her cheek'*) is a measure of how upset she is – that she is touched by such a simple gesture (from Alec of all people) emphasises her need for comfort ■ 'whit am I goin tae tell folks?' suggests despair, that she is lost, out of her depth ■ the pleading, despairing 'Oh Jenny, Jenny! Whit's happened tae ye, Jenny?' is emphasised by an exclamation followed by a question and by the almost lamenting tone from the repetition of her name ■ the stage direction *'Maggie looks helplessly on'* makes clear her vulnerability ■ *'combing her hair with her fingers'* is a visual indication of her misery.
	b)		2 marks may be awarded for detailed/insightful comment plus quotation/reference. 1 mark for more basic comment plus quotation/reference. 0 marks for quotation/reference alone. (Marks may be awarded 1+1.)	2	Possible answers include: ■ she is openly contemptuous of Alec: sneering language of 'tumphy' and 'big lump o dough' ■ she has a forceful personality: her dominance over Alec is seen when her sneering at his affection for his mother causes him to move away from her ■ her response when Lily says Alec is 'no as saft as he looks' is mock polite ('I'm right gled'), but really shows her contempt for Alec ■ her physical rejection of Alec '(*Pushing his face away*)' shows her attitude ■ 'but no for wee boys' is openly demeaning ■ her friendly comment when Jenny leaves ('Ta ta, Jenny. See you roon the toon') is rather provocative in face of others' disapproval.

Question			Expected response	Max. mark	Additional guidance

10			2 marks may be awarded for detailed/insightful comment plus quotation/reference.
			1 mark for more basic comment plus quotation/reference.
			0 marks for quotation/reference alone.
			(Marks may be awarded 2+2, 2+1+1 or 1+1+1+1.)
				4	Possible answers include:
					■ Jenny's low-key, undramatic 'Aye. Ta ta' is met with the unexpected arrival of her father, inevitably causing a tense moment
					■ the silent moments when they look at each other will be filled with tension
					■ John's anguish is described in the stage direction *Wretched*, which emphasises his distress for the audience
					■ the pathetic nature of his 'I thought ye'd hev gone' is countered by her offhand, monosyllabic, and far from friendly 'Naw. Jist gaun' which increases the tension between them
					■ the rest is entirely visual/aural; the lack of spoken words will concentrate the audience's attention on what they see and hear:
					  ■ a sign of defeat when John lowers his eyes and stands aside
					  ■ his wordless watching her could be defeat, longing, guilt
					  ■ the dying sound of footsteps emphasises her leaving
					  ■ the banging of the door concludes it.

11			Candidates can answer in bullet points in this final question, or write a number of linked statements. Marks for this question should be allocated following the guidelines given at the start of these Marking Instructions. See page 100.	10	Possible references include: ■ to begin with, she is hopelessly overburdened but is resigned to her role; by the end she is, to an extent, emancipated ■ at the start of the play she is very supportive of John; gives him his place and makes sure others do the same (e.g. her defence of him to Lily) ■ by the end she no longer subordinates herself to the needs (and weaknesses) of others ■ she makes a personal journey and becomes a stronger woman through the play, in many ways under the influence of the younger women in the play, e.g. she doesn't reject Jenny because of her lifestyle; even Isa teaches her that men can be weak ■ her journey reaches fruition at the end, when she stands up to John, humiliates him, accepts Jenny's money to enable the family to move to a healthier environment for Bertie, thus taking control of her own life and her family's future.

Text 1 – Prose – *The Red Door* by Iain Crichton Smith

Question			Expected response	Max. mark	Additional guidance
12			2 marks may be awarded for detailed/insightful comment plus quotation/reference. 1 mark for more basic comment plus quotation/reference. 0 marks for quotation/reference alone. (Marks may be awarded 2+2, 2+1+1 or 1+1+1+1.)	4	Possible answers include: ■ question 'But really was he happy?' shows uncertainty, doubt in his mind ■ repetition of 'He didn't like …' emphasises his dissatisfaction with current lifestyle ■ listing of the things he 'didn't like' shows how many things displeased him ■ 'that such and such … that that other one' hints at willingness to snipe at anyone ■ 'But the red door didn't do that': short affirmative sentence of how the red door represents the antithesis ■ colon introduces the key thing he feels is missing from his life – 'elegance' ■ 'Now Mary had elegance': short opening to new paragraph introduces the explanation of her 'elegance' ■ repetition of 'elegance' suggests its importance to him ■ use of concessionary words/expressions ('Though … It was true … And on the other hand') show him as being thoughtful, undogmatic ■ sequence of short sentences ('She seemed … She never … She was … She had …. She paid … She was') suggests he is enumerating her many qualities ■ 'But' at start of last sentence introduces her key quality.
13			2 marks may be awarded for detailed/insightful comment plus quotation/reference. 1 mark for more basic comment plus quotation/reference. 0 marks for quotation/reference alone. (Marks may be awarded 1+1.)	2	Possible answers include: ■ admires her generosity, altruism (care for children) ■ sees her as a free spirit ('walk by herself'), a little quixotic ('romantic') ■ prepared to see a usually negative quality ('sudden bursts of rage') in a positive way as a sign of her refusal to bend to anybody.
14			2 marks may be awarded for detailed/insightful comment plus quotation/reference. 1 mark for more basic comment plus quotation/reference.	4	Possible answers include: ■ 'seemed to be drawn inside it' suggests hypnotic powers ■ 'deep caves' suggests profound, unfathomable ■ 'all sorts of' suggests it is undefinable, mysterious

Question			Expected response	Max. mark	Additional guidance
			0 marks for quotation/reference alone. (Marks may be awarded 2+2, 2+1+1 or 1+1+1+1.)		■ 'veins and passages' suggests almost human ■ 'like a magic door …' suggests something out of a fairy-tale, enchanted ■ 'pulsed with a deep red light' suggests deliberately mesmerising, sci-fi overtones ■ 'make such a difference to house and moors and streams' suggests supernatural powers ■ 'sucked into it' suggests the door has physical power over him ■ 'a place of heat and colour and reality' suggests an inanimate object is vividly alive.
15			Candidates can answer in bullet points in this final question, or write a number of linked statements. Marks for this question should be allocated following the guidelines given at the start of these Marking Instructions. See page 100.	10	Possible references include: ■ *The Red Door* – pity for Murdo's sense of isolation in the village, his frustration at the narrowness of his existence ■ *The Telegram* – pity for both women because of the danger their sons are in, because of dread that the telegram is for her; pity for the elder ■ *In Church* – pity for the priest in his madness; pity for Colin's subjection to the priest's sermon and being killed ■ *The Crater* – pity for the soldiers having to cross No Man's Land, risking their lives, expending effort in vain ■ *The Painter* – pity for William after rejection by villagers; pity for narrator feeling forced into attacking William ■ *Mother and Son* – pity for son's having to endure nagging, having no life of his own.

Text 2 – Prose – *A Time to Keep* by George Mackay Brown

Question		Expected response	Max. mark	Additional guidance
16	a)	2 marks may be awarded for detailed/insightful comment plus quotation/reference. 1 mark for more basic comment plus quotation/reference. 0 marks for quotation/reference alone. (Marks may be awarded 1+1.)	2	Possible answers include: ■ absence of comment on the appearance of the first car on the island suggests he is unimpressed ■ 'watch-chain across his belly' – use of 'belly' draws attention to his unathletic appearance (unlike typical crofter); the mention of 'watch-chain' might suggest ostentation ■ 'stepping briskly' suggests purposeful, no nonsense ■ 'I was not beholden to him' – declares his independence, no sense of inferiority ■ 'and forby kirk elder, Justice of the Peace, chairman of the district council' – lists rather cynically how many positions of power/ authority Sinclair holds.

Question			Expected response	Max. mark	Additional guidance
16	b)		2 marks may be awarded for detailed/insightful comment plus quotation/reference. 1 mark for more basic comment plus quotation/reference. 0 marks for quotation/reference alone. (Marks may be awarded 1+1.)	2	Possible answers include: ■ the 'cry of distress' suggests she is afraid of him/intimidated by him ■ flurry of tidying up, emphasised by sentence structure/repeated pattern indicating frantic activity suggests she is desperate to impress/not to be thought ill of ■ straightening of the text suggests she is keen to demonstrate her religious credentials to him ■ covering Bill's anti-religious books shows she knows her father will disapprove and does not want to antagonise him.
	c)		2 marks may be awarded for detailed/insightful comment plus quotation/reference. 1 mark for more basic comment plus quotation/reference. 0 marks for quotation/reference alone. (Marks may be awarded 1+1.)	2	Possible answers include: ■ slightly cynical/disparaging – despite all her efforts, the house is little different ■ 'bed was unmade' suggests he thinks she doesn't even realise it hadn't been made ■ rather patronising 'She tried hard …' ■ 'not the tidiest of croft women' – litotes/understatement suggests he is aware of her shortcomings, but minimises criticism.
17			2 marks may be awarded for detailed/insightful comment plus quotation/reference. 1 mark for more basic comment plus quotation/reference. 0 marks for quotation/reference alone. (Marks may be awarded 2+2, 2+1+1 or 1+1+1+1.)	4	Possible answers include: ■ unlike the affectionate greeting for Ingi, Bill gets merely a 'well' ■ Bill replies in kind with a 'well' – almost cheekily repeating what Sinclair has said ■ Bill cuts across Sinclair's sympathy for Ingi by saying rather tartly 'On a croft … everybody must work', as if saying Ingi can't be treated softly ■ Sinclair's reply 'Is that so, Bill?' is fairly disrespectful, as if saying 'You must think I'm stupid if I don't know that …' ■ dismissive tone of 'Maybe so. At the present moment I'm speaking to Ingi …' ■ 'I'll be wanting to speak to you later' – peremptory tone, assuming he calls the shots ■ 'Say what you have to say now' – very abrupt, monosyllabic ■ Sinclair's sarcastic repetition of 'work' is designed to mock Bill ■ the aggressive, sort of finger-stabbing 'Eh?' ■ the belligerent 'Just answer me.' ■ 'Don't imagine I don't hear things' – asserting his superiority, perhaps threatening further revelations.

Question			Expected response	Max. mark	Additional guidance
18			Candidates can answer in bullet points in this final question, or write a number of linked statements. Marks for this question should be allocated following the guidelines given at the start of these Marking Instructions. See page 100.	10	Possible references include: ■ *A Time To Keep* – between Bill and: the other villagers at the start; Peter and John of Two Waters; Sinclair; the Orkney fishermen ■ *Tartan* – between the Vikings and the villagers; among the Vikings ■ *The Whaler's Return* – between Flaws and each character he meets; at the tinkers' wedding ■ *The Wireless Set* – in the reactions to Lord Haw Haw; uncertainty about accuracy of news; the arrival of the telegram ■ *The Eye of the Hurricane* – between Barclay and Stevens; between Barclay and Miriam; the presence of Stevens' old shipmates ■ *The Bright Spade* – at the meeting; when the group leave to search for food; the constant threat from the elements.

Text 3 – Prose – *The Trick Is To Keep Breathing* by Janice Galloway

Question			Expected response	Max. mark	Additional guidance
19			2 marks may be awarded for detailed/insightful comment plus quotation/reference. 1 mark for more basic comment plus quotation/reference. 0 marks for quotation/reference alone. (Marks may be awarded 2+2, 2+1+1 or 1+1+1+1.)	4	Possible answers include: ■ 'Asinine' suggests extreme stupidity ■ minor sentence 'My family' as if amused that he thinks she has any close family ■ 'little man' demeans not just stature but significance ■ 'dandruff' suggests lack of personal care ■ 'tortoise neck' compares him laughably with a less than imposing animal ■ 'clenched ... fists' suggests repressed anger ■ rhetorical question suggests he is incompetent ■ profanity 'for christsake' shows lack of respect ■ blunt, minor sentence 'He knew nothing' sums him up in just three words ■ 'paid to sit here' suggests she sees him as a mere functionary ■ 'say the first thing that came into his bald head' suggests he has no professional competence ■ 'meaningless nothings' suggests his work is pointless ■ 'complete stranger' suggests he has no interest in her ■ 'arteries on my wrist throbbed, pulsing' shows the physical effect he has on her ■ 'like an empty tiger' suggests he has aroused animal aggressiveness in her.

Question			Expected response	Max. mark	Additional guidance
20			2 marks may be awarded for detailed/insightful comment plus quotation/reference. 1 mark for more basic comment plus quotation/reference. 0 marks for quotation/reference alone. (Marks may be awarded 2+2, 2+1+1 or 1+1+1+1.)	4	Possible answers include: <ul><li>question 'Didn't he know?' suggests frustration at his question</li><li>'stuck in this stuffy room in the corner' suggests she sees herself as marginalised</li><li>'equally absurd stranger' – she sees herself as ridiculous</li><li>'hiding from the sun' misrepresents the simple fact of being indoors</li><li>'The sky was passing outside'– a surreal description which distorts reality</li><li>'for chrissakes' – moved to swear by her situation</li><li>'Planes and birds. People going about their work' – two flat minor sentences as if enumerating what she's missing</li><li>'The whole thing was insane' – exaggeration as she tries to sum up the situation</li><li>'bits got stuck on the way out' – a disturbing description of a simple process</li><li>'it was just a blur' – no longer able to take in what is being said</li><li>'Tears drained backward into my ears' – bizarre dislocation of eyes/ears</li><li>'floating up toward the ceiling' – suggests some kind of out-of-body experience</li><li>'serene and distant as the Virgin Mary, radiating Truth from the halo of stars round my head' – creates a fantastic, religious image of herself as if no longer part of the real world.</li></ul>
21			2 marks may be awarded for detailed/insightful comment plus quotation/reference. 1 mark for more basic comment plus quotation/reference. 0 marks for quotation/reference alone. (Marks may be awarded 1+1.)	2	Possible answers include: <ul><li>she has reached complete disillusion with the doctor</li><li>she feels she has reached a superior plane of knowledge</li><li>she sees herself as superior to him</li><li>as if she has experienced mystical, spiritual insight into the meaning of life</li><li>written in the form of gnomic statements – simple sentences, capital letters at key words – as if universal truths</li><li>totally nihilistic outlook.</li></ul>

Question			Expected response	Max. mark	Additional guidance
22			Candidates can answer in bullet points in this final question, or write a number of linked statements. Marks for this question should be allocated following the guidelines given at the start of these Marking Instructions. See page 100.	10	Possible references include: ■ frequent 'out-of-body experiences' – as in extract (NB opening line: 'I watch myself from the corner of the room'); as if she is observing her illness with us as readers; loss of identity ■ totally isolated; lacks any social role as wife, daughter, mother, mistress ■ no effective connection with any of the health professionals (Doctors One, Two and Three; Health Visitor) ■ frequent use of script form suggests she is part of a play, not her 'real' self ■ feels at odds with bureaucracy (Mr Dick, school management) ■ 'relationship' with Tony – she is aware of his repulsiveness, but succumbs to his advances ■ her detachment from (and fear of) Myra ■ retreats into a fixation with lists, dates, etc. as a way of surviving her depression ■ absence of emotion – past intense situations are described, but there is an aloofness, a coolness in her descriptions of events in the present ■ irony in idea that the only person she can communicate with (Marianne) is thousands of miles away.

Text 4 – Prose – *Sunset Song* by Lewis Grassic Gibbon

Question			Expected response	Max. mark	Additional guidance
23			2 marks may be awarded for detailed/insightful comment plus quotation/reference. 1 mark for more basic comment plus quotation/reference. 0 marks for quotation/reference alone. (Marks may be awarded 2+2, 2+1+1 or 1+1+1+1.)	4	Possible answers include: ■ 'sneered' suggests contempt in his voice ■ *Hell, Chris, what a bloody place!'* – the coarse language suggests a lack of respect ■ 'flung his pack one way and his hat the other' suggests a lack of care, self-respect ■ 'as though she were a tink' compares Chris to someone to be looked down on, of no value ■ 'hot and questing and wise' suggests he is being sexually aggressive, selfish, that he is more experienced now than he was and isn't afraid to make Chris aware of it ■ 'the hot smoulder fire in his eyes' suggests he is almost demonic, malevolent ■ 'red with other things' suggests he is sexually aroused in a frightening way ■ *Well, we'll hope so, eh Chris?'* – crude, sexual innuendo

Question			Expected response	Max. mark	Additional guidance
					■ *'unless you're too bloody stand-offish'* – open insult to his wife coarsened by use of offensive language ■ 'picked the thing up and flung it ...' – such lack of respect for his own child's picture book (emphasised by 'thing' and 'flung') is an especially upsetting detail ■ the commanding tone of *'Here, give us some tea'* as if Chris were a servant to be bossed about.
24			2 marks may be awarded for detailed/insightful comment plus quotation/reference. 1 mark for more basic comment plus quotation/reference. 0 marks for quotation/reference alone. (Marks may be awarded 2+2, 2+1+1 or 1+1+1+1.)	4	Possible answers include: ■ 'like a beast at a trough' suggests she sees him as non-human, merely satisfying basic needs, no self-respect; the harsh, plosive consonants at 'beast' and 'trough' add a hint of disgust ■ 'coarse hair that sprang like short bristles' suggests she sees him as rough, unrefined, compares him with an inanimate object ■ 'red and angry circle about the collar' shows that she can sense his aggressiveness in the chafing left by his uniform ■ 'a great half-healed scar ... glinted putrescent blue' – a revolting description of something deeply unhealthy, unnatural, almost alive.
25			2 marks may be awarded for detailed/insightful comment plus quotation/reference. 1 mark for more basic comment plus quotation/reference. 0 marks for quotation/reference alone. (Marks may be awarded 1+1.)	2	Possible answers include: ■ at first, he is cautious, but acknowledges Ewan as his father, albeit with little or no emotion: 'just said *It's father.*' ■ at the end he is scared/seeks Chris's protection, calling him 'that soldier', i.e. denying any relationship.
26			Candidates can answer in bullet points in this final question, or write a number of linked statements. Marks for this question should be allocated following the guidelines given at the start of these Marking Instructions. See page 100.	10	Possible references include: ■ the initial wooing – nervous, occasionally comic ■ early passion, happy domestic life with Chris and young Ewan ■ problems emerge (e.g. his temper when asked about Sarah Sinclair) ■ Chris's growing sense that Ewan doesn't understand her (e.g. over the 'realm of the dead') ■ the disparity in intellect (e.g. his attitude to history at Dunnottar Castle) ■ the disagreements about going to war; his treatment of her on his leave; the report from Chae about his love for her at the end; her vision of him after his death.

Text 5 – Prose – *The Cone-Gatherers* by Robin Jenkins

Question			Expected response	Max. mark	Additional guidance
27			2 marks may be awarded for detailed/insightful comment plus quotation/reference. 1 mark for more basic comment plus quotation/reference. 0 marks for quotation/reference alone. (Marks may be awarded 2+2, 2+1+1 or 1+1+1+1.)	4	Possible answers include: ■ 'thrilling as a pipe lament' suggests uplifting, musical, emotional ■ 'daylight announced' – personification suggests power of nature ■ 'a last blaze of light' suggests sudden burst of powerful sunlight ■ 'an uncanny clarity' suggests almost mystical sense of brightness ■ 'splendour and puissance' suggests magnificence and power ■ 'abdication' suggests a grand, important change as in a monarch stepping down ■ alliteration in 'Single stars' adds poetic weight to the description ■ 'glittering' suggests brightness, attractiveness ■ unusual, old-fashioned word order in 'a sky pale and austere' adds a sense of gravity, importance ■ 'Dusk like a breathing' – synaesthesia makes the moment seem dreamlike, unworldly ■ 'drifted ... crept' suggests stealthy, gentle, peaceful ■ periodic structure of the sentence 'Slowly ... became indistinguishable' lists all the different colours and climaxes in the idea of their merging into one ■ 'mottled yellow ... bronze ... saffron' creates a palette of soft colours ■ 'sombre harmonies of decay' – a highly poetic image of the beauty of nature ■ 'Owls hooted. A fox barked' – the two short sentences focus on sound and create a haunting mood.
28			2 marks may be awarded for detailed/insightful comment plus quotation/reference. 1 mark for more basic comment plus quotation/reference. 0 marks for quotation/reference alone. (Marks may be awarded 1+1.)	2	Possible answers include: ■ an almost telepathic understanding: nothing is said, but they seem to know what each other is doing ■ clearly, if unspoken, defined roles: Calum will lead the way down the tree, and help Neil ■ implicit understanding, trust in each other: Calum doesn't ask what Neil is thinking, but their being together is all he asks.

Question			Expected response	Max. mark	Additional guidance
29			2 marks may be awarded for detailed/insightful comment plus quotation/reference. 1 mark for more basic comment plus quotation/reference. 0 marks for quotation/reference alone. (Marks may be awarded 2+2, 2+1+1 or 1+1+1+1.)	4	Possible answers include: ■ patience: waits for 'about half an hour' without complaint ■ one-ness with nature: 'fancied he was resting in the heart of an enormous flower' ■ love of nature: 'as he breathed in the fragrance' ■ tenderness: 'he stroked the branches, and to his gentle hands they were as soft as petals' ■ child-like imagination: 'as if he was an owl himself' ■ complete absorption in the fantasy: 'He became an owl himself …' ■ awareness of suffering in nature: 'he suffered in the ineluctable predicament of necessary pain and death' ■ inability to understand suffering in nature: 'This was the terrifying mystery' ■ detachment from world events: 'he tried, with success, to forget it' ■ contentment with what he has: '"I could sit up here all night …" … assured him eagerly'.
30			Candidates can answer in bullet points in this final question, or write a number of linked statements. Marks for this question should be allocated following the guidelines given at the start of these Marking Instructions. See page 100.	10	Possible references include: ■ constant comparisons with nature (especially birds) ■ inability to understand Duror's hatred ■ desire to help the injured rabbit; confusion/inner-conflict about death in nature ■ doesn't share/understand Neil's resentment of the aristocracy ■ doesn't mind being stared at by Roderick and Sheila 'as if you were a monkey' ■ not upset by the child on the bus ■ his concern for the cones when the storm breaks ■ doesn't take part in the exclusion of the conscientious objectors in Lendrick ■ child-like attraction to the broken doll ■ defence of Neil in beach hut ■ the 'innocence' of his death; comparisons with crucifixion.

Text 1 – Poetry – *A Poet's Welcome to His Love-Begotten Daughter* by Robert Burns

Question			Expected response	Max. mark	Additional guidance

31			For full marks both the daughter and the critics should be covered but not necessarily in equal measure.
			
			2 marks may be awarded for detailed/insightful comment plus quotation/reference.
			
			1 mark for more basic comment plus quotation/reference.
			
			0 marks for quotation/reference alone.
			
			(Marks may be awarded 2+2, 2+1+1 or 1+1+1+1.)
				4	Possible answers include:
					
					■ Attitude to daughter – love, affection, pride:
					  ■ informal 'Thou's'
					  ■ 'welcome' – she is openly and warmly received
					  ■ wishes ill on himself ('mishanter') if he thinks of her badly
					  ■ 'My bonie lady' – playfully grants her title of 'lady'
					  ■ happy, not ashamed to be called by childish names 'Tyta or daddie'.
					
					■ Attitude to critics – defiant, defensive, contemptuous:
					  ■ 'Tho' now …' implies he is not concerned at what they call him
					  ■ use of 'they' suggests a contempt in not defining them
					  ■ 'fornicator' is a particularly strong word, suggesting the strength of their criticism
					  ■ 'kintry clatter' – alliteration mimics the harsh sound of their chatter
					  ■ 'clatter' – onomatopoeia mimics noisy gossip
					  ■ 'let them clash' – dismissive tone
					  ■ 'clash' – suggests pointless, aimless chatter
					  ■ 'auld wife's' – dismisses his critics as old women
					  ■ 'feckless' suggests puny, silly
					  ■ 'gie ane fash' – not even worth a single worry.

32			2 marks may be awarded for detailed/insightful comment plus quotation/reference. 1 mark for more basic comment plus quotation/reference. 0 marks for quotation/reference alone. (Marks may be awarded 1+1.)	2	Possible answers include: ■ the exclamatory interjection 'Welcome!' reinforces his defiance of the criticism in the previous stanza ■ 'bonie, sweet, wee dochter,' piles up a list of the many reasons to love her ■ 'Tho' ye … tho' your' concedes possible reasons for criticism; they will almost inevitably be followed by 'Yet …' ■ parenthetical 'by my faith' asserts his strength of feeling ■ 'That I shall swear!' – short robust declaration of intent.

Question			Expected response	Max. mark	Additional guidance
33			2 marks may be awarded for detailed/insightful comment plus quotation/reference. 1 mark for more basic comment plus quotation/reference. 0 marks for quotation/reference alone. (Marks may be awarded 2+2, 2+1+1 or 1+1+1+1.)	4	Possible answers include: ■ compares her with her mother whom he calls 'bonie' ■ 'fatherly' implies he feels a loving bond ■ 'daut' suggests handling gently and lovingly ■ the rhyme 'dear ... near' adds a gentle, musical touch ■ prepared to defend her against criticism from the whole church ■ 'Sweet fruit' suggests something natural, attractive, wholesome ■ 'mony a merry dint' recalls with pleasure (heightened by the alliteration) the activities which led to her conception ■ those who would 'scoff' at her birth are dismissed as 'fools' ■ asserts that he will support her to the 'last plack', i.e. the tiniest remaining coin.
34			Candidates can answer in bullet points in this final question, or write a number of linked statements. Marks for this question should be allocated following the guidelines given at the start of these Marking Instructions. See page 100.	10	Possible references include: ■ *A Poet's Welcome* – contrasts his love with others' condemnation; contrasts his free spirit with the narrow-mindedness of others ■ *Tam o' Shanter* – contrasts the bonhomie in the tavern with the terrors outside; contrasts men's stupidity with women's common sense; contrast in use of Scots and English ■ *To a Mouse* – contrasts 'Man's dominion' and 'nature's social union'; contrasts hopes and reality ■ *A Man's a Man for a' That* – contrasts aristocratic rank with 'the honest man'; contrasts outward show with inner worth; contrasts 'coward slave' with 'the man o independent mind' ■ *Holy Willie's Prayer* – contrasts impression HW is trying to create with the reality; contrasts genuine prayer with the travesty that is HW's spiteful, self-promoting effort ■ *Address to the Deil* – contrasts traditional awesome Devil of the Bible (and Milton) with a Devil who is more of a likeable rogue.

Text 2 – Poetry – *Mrs Midas* by Carol Ann Duffy

Question	Expected response	Max. mark	Additional guidance
35	2 marks may be awarded for detailed/insightful comment plus quotation/reference. 1 mark for more basic comment plus quotation/reference. 0 marks for quotation/reference alone. (Marks may be awarded 2+2, 2+1+1 or 1+1+1+1.)	**4**	Possible answers include: ■ the use of simple statement 'It was late September', as if recounting a simple recollection ■ the use of informal contraction 'I'd just poured' suggests relaxed tone ■ the absence of 'and' between 'wine' and 'begun' is informal, sounds comfortable ■ everyday detail ('a glass of wine') suggests relaxation, contentment ■ word choice of 'unwind' suggests calmness, composure ■ imagery/personification of 'The kitchen/filled with the smell of itself' suggests warmth, pleasant smells, promise of good food ■ 'steamy breath/gently blanching the windows' – personification of kitchen as something alive, warm, tender ■ conversational tone of 'So I opened one' as if continuing a simple story ■ 'wiped the other's glass like a brow' – affectionate, caring, unthreatening gesture ■ simple description of what husband is doing 'standing under the pear tree ...' ■ 'snapping a twig' suggests a small, unthreatening action.
36	2 marks may be awarded for detailed/insightful comment plus quotation/reference. 1 mark for more basic comment plus quotation/reference. 0 marks for quotation/reference alone. (Marks may be awarded 1+1.)	**2**	Possible answers include: ■ tone of 'Now the garden was long and the visibility poor' – as if offering an excuse for possibly not seeing correctly ■ the imagery of 'the dark of the ground seems to drink the light of the sky' suggests something mysterious, dark, deprived of light, uncertain ■ the delayed assertion 'but that twig in his hand was gold' as if unwilling to state what she is seeing ■ the parenthetical '– we grew Fondante d'Automne –' seems an unnecessary detail as if trying to hold onto reality by including it ■ the minor sentence 'On' conveys a sense of stupefaction, unable to say anything more than a single syllable ■ question 'Is he putting fairy lights in the tree?' suggests doubt, almost an attempt to rationalise.

Question			Expected response	Max. mark	Additional guidance
37			2 marks may be awarded for detailed/insightful comment plus quotation/reference. 1 mark for more basic comment plus quotation/reference. 0 marks for quotation/reference alone. (Marks may be awarded 2+2, 2+1+1 or 1+1+1+1.)	4	Possible answers include: ■ the juxtaposition of the ordinary ('He came into the house') with the extraordinary ('The doorknobs gleamed') ■ the way his behaviour causes her mind to jump to a schoolroom memory ■ the simile 'like a king on a burnished throne' presents him as a regal figure amid great splendour ■ 'strange, wild, vain' – use of three monosyllables to convey a wide range of emotions ■ 'He started to laugh' suggests an almost irrational response to the situation ■ 'spitting out the teeth of the rich' – a grotesque image combining pain/discomfort with association of wealth ■ structure of 'toyed with his spoon, then mine, then with the knives, the forks' suggests random actions, as if he is confused ■ 'glass, goblet, golden chalice' shows the progression from simple drinking vessel to exotic 'chalice'; emphasised by the alliteration ■ structure of 'picked up the glass, goblet, golden chalice, drank' – suggests staccato movement, unusual behaviour.
38			Candidates can answer in bullet points in this final question, or write a number of linked statements. Marks for this question should be allocated following the guidelines given at the start of these Marking Instructions. See page 100.	10	Possible references include: ■ *Mrs Midas* – the updated version of the Midas legend; the speaker's attitude to her husband; a number of the specific details, e.g. 'spitting out the teeth of the rich' ■ *Havisham* – the dramatic, apparently contradictory opening words; the depth of her antipathy and the hints of sexual violence; the 'corpse'/'honeymoon' paradox ■ *Anne Hathaway* – the extravagant imagery; the revisionist take on 'second best bed'; her suggestion that her husband is 'living' ■ *Valentine* – the rejection of the conventional love message; the surprise of 'I give you an onion'; the association of love and violence ■ *War Photographer* – the idea of the photographer as priest; the impact of the horrors in the war zones; the complacency of 'rural England'; the cynical approach of the editor ■ *Originally* – the surreal imagery of the 'room/which fell through fields'; the notion of childhood as an 'emigration'; the idea of culture etc. being lost/replaced.

Text 3 – Poetry – *Some Old Photographs* by Liz Lochhead

Question			Expected response	Max. mark	Additional guidance
39			2 marks may be awarded for detailed/insightful comment plus quotation/reference. 1 mark for more basic comment plus quotation/reference. 0 marks for quotation/reference alone. (Marks may be awarded 2+2, 2+1+1 or 1+1+1+1.)	4	Possible answers include: ■ the lack of punctuation/the ungrammatical nature of each line creates a muddled, dreamlike impression; it's like one enormous list of impressions ■ the uneven, irregular lines give it a distorted, random feel ■ the synaesthesia in 'weather evocative as scent' suggests a confusion, in which something inanimate can be described as strong, lingering ■ paradox in 'romance of dark stormclouds' describes what is usually seen as threatening ('stormclouds') in terms of pleasure, passion ■ stress pattern in 'low wide river', three consecutive long vowel sounds creates a heavy, slowed down effect ■ word play in 'long ... and longer' suggests confusion, uncertainty (+ hint of 'long' = yearning) ■ the enjambment in 'of light/of smoke' draws out the sound as if one image is piling up on another ■ 'fabulous film-noir stills' conjures up images of stylish Hollywood movies; also suggests a hint of menace, that anything can happen ■ slightly incongruous comparison of Central Station with Hollywood chic ■ the repeated 'f' sound in 'fabulous ... film ... freezing ... fog' creates an echo effect ■ assonance and rhyme in 'silvering the chilled, stilled' continues the echo effect ■ 'the glamorous past' suggests a world/time where everything was stylish, no flaws or problems ■ metaphor of 'drops on a rainmate are sequins' turn something prosaic ('rainmate') into something dazzling, sophisticated.
40			2 marks may be awarded for detailed/insightful comment plus quotation/reference. 1 mark for more basic comment plus quotation/reference. 0 marks for quotation/reference alone.	2	Possible answers include: ■ 'still-lovely mother' indicates the photograph shows the mother before she aged/lost her youthful beauty ■ 'before you were born' as if the poet is talking to herself about a very distant time ■ reference to 'all' dads being 'in hats' must be a time (1950s at the latest?) when all adult males wore hats

Question			Expected response	Max. mark	Additional guidance
			(Marks may be awarded 1+1.)		<ul><li>'Central at five past five' suggests a bygone time when all offices and businesses closed at five o'clock</li><li>'belted dark overcoats' suggest, again, the 1950s or earlier.</li></ul>
41			2 marks may be awarded for detailed/insightful comment plus quotation/reference. 1 mark for more basic comment plus quotation/reference. 0 marks for quotation/reference alone. (Marks may be awarded 2+2, 2+1+1 or 1+1+1+1.)	4	Possible answers include: <ul><li>'starlings swarming' suggests a sense of movement/bustle</li><li>'noise and stink and smoky breath' suggests a sense of urban grit</li><li>the list 'all the passing now/and noise and stink and smoky breath' suggests a sense of relentless activity</li><li>'above what was/never really this photograph' suggests a slightly surreal impression – as if the photograph has vanished and she is/thinks she is actually in the Square.</li></ul>
42			Candidates can answer in bullet points in this final question, or write a number of linked statements. Marks for this question should be allocated following the guidelines given at the start of these Marking Instructions. See page 100.	10	Possible references include: <ul><li>*Some Old Photographs* – despite their nostalgic associations the photographs seem to represent the inexorable passage of time ('what was/never really this photograph'); the importance of the future in 'that boat is yet to sail'</li><li>*Last Supper* – explores the fate of past relationships with amusing relish, but emphasises the need to look to the future ('get hungry/and go hunting again')</li><li>*For My Grandmother Knitting* – affectionate recollection of grandmother is set against the grandchildren's rejection of her gifts ('now they say there is no need'); idea at end of life having passed the grandmother by</li><li>*My Rival's House* – touches on the passage of time within the mother/son relationship ('This son she bore ...') and the mother's unwillingness/inability to accept that her son has grown up ('fight foul for her survival')</li><li>*The Bargain* – explores the passage of time within a relationship; the significance of the time of year ('January ... looking back, looking forward') as a crucial moment; the desire either to mend the past or give up and look forwards: 'I wish we could either mend things/or learn to throw them away'</li><li>*View of Scotland/Love Poem* – looks back to past Hogmanays and their promise of better things to come in terms of the speaker's relationship(s).</li></ul>

Text 4 – Poetry – *Memorial* by Norman MacCaig

Question			Expected response	Max. mark	Additional guidance
43			2 marks may be awarded for detailed/insightful comment plus quotation/reference. 1 mark for more basic comment plus quotation/reference. 0 marks for quotation/reference alone. (Marks may be awarded 1+1.)	2	Possible answers include: ■ 'The silence of her dying sounds through/ the carousel of language' compares silence with something that can make a sound, suggesting confusion or heightened awareness of her absence; compares language to a carousel – something associated with joyful sound and happy experiences, suggesting she is felt/sensed at all times, albeit in an incongruous way ■ 'It's a web/on which laughter stitches itself' compares the silence with an intricate pattern, and imagines laughter as capable of attaching itself to the web, suggesting her presence/absence is capable of causing happiness ('laughter'), an apparently contradictory emotion.
44			2 marks may be awarded for detailed/insightful comment plus quotation/reference. 1 mark for more basic comment plus quotation/reference. 0 marks for quotation/reference alone. (Marks may be awarded 2+2, 2+1+1 or 1+1+1+1.)	4	Possible answers include: ■ various contrasts of living/dying suggest confusion, unwillingness to accept the death ■ contrast of the vivid and natural ('bird … sun … fish … crocus') with sense of death, emptiness ('black words … the sound/of soundlessness … nowhere') ■ contrast between what 'she tells …' and what 'I hear …' suggests he is living with both happiness and sadness ■ contrast between beauty of 'No crocus is carved more gently' and the bleakness of 'the nowhere/she is continuously going into' shows the persona feels the death in a contradictory way ■ contrast/contradiction in 'sound/of soundlessness' suggests confusion, or a heightened awareness of the absence.
45			2 marks may be awarded for detailed/insightful comment plus quotation/reference. 1 mark for more basic comment plus quotation/reference. 0 marks for quotation/reference alone. (Marks may be awarded 2+2, 2+1+1 or 1+1+1+1.)	4	Possible answers include: ■ he says she 'can't stop dying' – in his mind he relives her death all the time ■ she has the power to make him 'her elegy' – he personifies everything he would want to say about her death ■ the extended 'artistic' metaphor ('elegy … masterpiece … fiction … music') creates an elaborate sense of how her death/memory permeates every aspect of his life and his creativity

Question			Expected response	Max. mark	Additional guidance
					▪ the apparently contradictory nature of 'walking masterpiece' and 'true fiction' suggests bewilderment, disorientation ▪ the enigmatic last line suggests they have almost merged in personality.
46			Candidates can answer in bullet points in this final question, or write a number of linked statements. Marks for this question should be allocated following the guidelines given at the start of these Marking Instructions. See page 100.	10	Possible references include: ▪ *Memorial* – the idea of being haunted/surrounded by the loved one ('Everywhere ...'); the depth of his sense of loss ('the nowhere/she is continuously going into') ▪ *Visiting hour* – the difficulty in controlling emotions ('I will not feel ...'); the sense of loss ('the distance of pain ...') ▪ *Sounds of the Day* – the enormity of the separation ('the end/of all the sounds there are'); the pain caused by the separation ('the whole hand goes numb') ▪ *Assisi* – the deep emotion in the description of the dwarf's deformities ('slumped like a half-filled sack', 'whose eyes/wept pus'); the contempt for the priest and the tourists ▪ *Basking shark* – the frightening realisation of his own smallness in the scheme of things ('The thought made me grow pale') ▪ *Aunt Julia* – sadness at his inability to communicate ('so many questions unanswered').

Text 5 – Poetry – *Hallaig* by Sorley MacLean

Question			Expected response	Max. mark	Additional guidance
47	a)		1 mark for each appropriate identification. 0 marks for quotation/reference alone.	2	Possible answers include: ▪ the influence of the past ▪ the confluence of past and present (and future) ▪ the landscape of Hallaig/Raasay ▪ the poet's sense of connection to the history of the community ▪ a celebration of tradition and heritage.
	b)		2 marks may be awarded for detailed/insightful comment plus quotation/reference. 1 mark for more basic comment plus quotation/reference.	4	Possible answers include: ▪ use of possessive 'my' shows sense of belonging, identity ▪ 'Norman and big Hector' – use of Christian names/nickname suggests familiarity, friendship

Question			Expected response	Max. mark	Additional guidance
			0 marks for quotation/ reference alone. (Marks may be awarded 2+2, 2+1+1 or 1+1+1+1.)		▪ 'their daughters and their sons are a wood' connects generations to natural growth, organic development, continuity ▪ dislike/criticism of non-native species ('pine') seen as 'proud', 'crowing' ▪ 'birch wood' as the natural, preferred species – poet is prepared to wait for it, sees it as something that will eventually provide comfort ('shade' for the whole area).
48			2 marks may be awarded for detailed/insightful comment plus quotation/reference. 1 mark for more basic comment plus quotation/ reference. 0 marks for quotation/ reference alone. (Marks may be awarded 2+2, 2+1+1 or 1+1+1+1.)	4	Possible answers include: ▪ 'Sabbath of the dead' suggests an ongoing, present-day celebration of the dead ▪ 'people are frequenting' suggests current presence, movement, community; use of present tense makes it appear to be happening now ▪ 'every single generation gone' emphasises extent of past destruction ▪ 'They are still in Hallaig' – unambiguous assertion of presence ▪ 'MacLeans and MacLeods' – use of local names in the plural suggests continuity across many generations ▪ 'all who were there' – past tense draws attention to what is gone ▪ 'the dead have been seen alive' – direct reference to the past in the present; clear contrast of 'dead' and 'alive' ▪ absence of verb in final stanza creates ambiguity ▪ 'men lying' suggests death ▪ 'girls a wood of birches' suggests no longer alive as people, but alive in nature ▪ 'straight their backs' suggests alive, proud ▪ 'bent their heads' suggests mourning.
49			Candidates can answer in bullet points in this final question, or write a number of linked statements. Marks for this question should be allocated following the guidelines given at the start of these Marking Instructions. See page 100.	10	Possible references include: ▪ *Hallaig* – reflects on Hallaig as it was and as it is now ('They are still in Hallaig,/ MacLeans and MacLeods'); it both laments and celebrates a once-thriving community and way of life, displaced by the Highland Clearances ▪ *Screapadal* – the abandoned township of Screapadal is used to describe the destruction of community during the Highland Clearances, and the threat of total devastation from nuclear weapons ▪ *Shores* – a sense of various places (Talisker, Calgary, Moidart) are part of a timeless landscape, of powerful natural forces

Question			Expected response	Max. mark	Additional guidance
					• *I gave you immortality* – celebrates the tradition of the inspired poet tortured by lost love; references to 'the Land of Youth', 'the high wood of the men of song', 'the Deluge' place it firmly in a mythical/biblical context • *Heroes* – reference to historical heroes ('Lannes at Ratisbon …') and the traditions of heroism, provides a historical context for the contrast/comparison with the 'poor little chap', and for the reflections on the horrors of war.

Text 6 – Poetry – *Nil Nil* by Don Paterson

Question			Expected response	Max. mark	Additional guidance
50			2 marks may be awarded for detailed/insightful comment plus quotation/reference. 1 mark for more basic comment plus quotation/reference. 0 marks for quotation/reference alone. (Marks may be awarded 2+2, 2+1+1 or 1+1+1+1.)	4	Possible answers include: • the sentence structure (long, rambling list, dominated by 'then') suggests an almost endless, unstoppable process • the ironic reference to their one success as a 'setback' suggests just how inexorable the decline actually was • 'fifty-year slide' suggest the decline lasted for a long time, and was relentless • 'Sunday League' suggests second-rate, not comparable with serious Saturday games • 'big tartan flasks' suggests refreshments brought from home, not provided by the club • 'open hatchbacks' suggests players have driven themselves right up to the pitch, no team transport • 'half-time satsuma' suggests very limited, frugal nourishment provided • 'the dog on the pitch' is slightly humorous, suggests a ground where no one pays much attention • 'Boy's Club' implies it has lost senior status • 'then nobody' is a bleak description of the end of sponsorship • spectators are reduced to 'grim fathers' (no enjoyment) and 'perverts' (disturbing image of people there for the wrong reason).
51			2 marks may be awarded for detailed/insightful comment plus quotation/reference. 1 mark for more basic comment plus quotation/reference. 0 marks for quotation/reference alone. (Marks may be awarded 2+2, 2+1+1 or 1+1+1+1.)	4	Possible answers include: • 'unrefereed thirty-a-sides' suggests chaotic, anarchic • 'terrified' suggests the lame boys have been bullied into their roles • 'fat boys with callipers' suggests the insensitive language used by others • 'infinite, notional fields' suggests the lack of order, control • 'dwindling' suggests steady decline, loss of status

Question			Expected response	Max. mark	Additional guidance
					■ 'half-hearted' suggests lack of enthusiasm
					■ 'kickabouts' suggests informal, unstructured, without any passion
					■ 'so smelly the air seems to quiver above him' – the description of Horace is vivid and direct
					■ 'desperate' suggests frantic, uncontrolled
					■ 'bald tennis ball' suggests over-used, well past its usefulness
					■ 'the hour before lighting-up time' symbolises approaching dark.
52			2 marks may be awarded for detailed/insightful comment plus quotation/reference. 1 mark for more basic comment plus quotation/ reference. 0 marks for quotation/ reference alone. (Marks may be awarded 1+1.)	2	Possible answers include: ■ his being left alone by someone who 'cheats' ■ 'hack up' suggests the process is clumsy, crude, inelegant ■ 'in the rain' – pathetic fallacy to suggest misery ■ 'stopped swings' suggests the park is deserted, implying loneliness, isolation ■ 'dead shanty-town' suggests the area he lives in is run-down, almost primitive ■ 'black shell' suggests environment is dark, dirty, empty ■ 'cul-de-sac' symbolises a dead-end existence ■ the pathetic attempt to 'swank off' after a mere fluke.
53			Candidates can answer in bullet points in this final question, or write a number of linked statements. Marks for this question should be allocated following the guidelines given at the start of these Marking Instructions. See page 100.	10	Possible references include: ■ *Nil Nil* – the decline of the football club ('fifty-year slide'); the change in the area and in the recreation ground ('ten years of dwindling') ■ *The Thread* – time allows the change from frailty at birth to healthy child, part of a united family ■ *Waking With Russell* – change over time in father/speaker as he comes to terms with being a father ■ *The Ferryman's Arms* – idea of passing time in the pub playing pool while waiting for the ferry is symbolically linked to the passage of life, awaiting death ■ *Two Trees* – distinct stages in the history of the trees over time adds to the apparent simplicity of the fable (which is not a fable) ■ *11.00: Baldovan* – specific time in title points to significance of time in our lives; passage of time during the journey; change in focus from simple shopping trip to mysterious return; the time-shift such that 'sisters and mothers are fifty years dead'.

Section 2 – Critical Essay – 20 marks

Supplementary marking grid

	Marks 20–19	Marks 18–16	Marks 15–13	Marks 12–10	Marks 9–6	Marks 5–0
Knowledge and understanding **The critical essay demonstrates:**	thorough knowledge and understanding of the text	secure knowledge and understanding of the text	clear knowledge and understanding of the text	adequate knowledge and understanding of the text	limited evidence of knowledge and understanding of the text	very little knowledge and understanding of the text
	perceptive selection of textual evidence to support line of argument which is fluently structured and expressed	detailed textual evidence to support line of thought which is coherently structured and expressed	clear textual evidence to support line of thought which is clearly structured and expressed	adequate textual evidence to support line of thought which is adequately structured and expressed	limited textual evidence to support line of thought which is structured and expressed in a limited way	very little textual evidence to support line of thought which shows very little structure or clarity of expression
	perceptive focus on the demands of the question	secure focus on the demands of the question	clear focus on the demands of the question	adequate focus on the demands of the question	limited focus on the demands of the question	very little focus on the demands of the question
Analysis **The critical essay demonstrates:**	perceptive analysis of the effect of features of language/filmic techniques	detailed analysis of the effect of features of language/filmic techniques	clear analysis of the effect of features of language/filmic techniques	adequate analysis of the effect of features of language/filmic techniques	limited analysis of the effect of features of language/filmic techniques	very little analysis of features of language/filmic techniques
Evaluation **The critical essay demonstrates:**	committed evaluative stance with respect to the text and the task	engaged evaluative stance with respect to the text and the task	clear evaluative stance with respect to the text and the task	adequate evidence of an evaluative stance with respect to the text and the task	limited evidence of an evaluative stance with respect to the text and the task	very little evidence of an evaluative stance with respect to the text and the task
Technical Accuracy **The critical essay demonstrates:**	few errors in spelling, grammar, sentence construction, punctuation and paragraphing the ability to be understood at first reading		clear focus on demands of the question	adequate focus on the demands of the question	significant number of errors in spelling, grammar, sentence construction, punctuation and paragraphing which impedes understanding	

Practice Paper B

Paper 1: Reading for Understanding, Analysis and Evaluation

Passage 1

Question			Expected response	Max. mark	Additional guidance
1	a)		Candidates must use their own words. No marks for straight lifts from the passage. 1 mark for each point from the 'Additional guidance' column.	4	Possible answers include: ■ he encountered a huge amount of choice in several consumer situations ■ abundance of choice is especially noticeable in the USA ■ he was baffled, overwhelmed by the amount of choice ■ family disagreements arose from the range of products available ■ he was unable to make choices ■ he wasn't able to avoid making choices ■ his refusal to choose was met with astonishment ■ he (almost) lost his temper in one situation.
	b)		For full marks there should be comments on at least two examples. 2 marks may be awarded for detailed/insightful comment plus quotation/reference. 1 mark for more basic comment plus quotation/reference. 0 marks for quotation/reference alone. (Marks may be awarded 2+2, 2+1+1 or 1+1+1+1.)	4	Possible answers include: ■ the exaggeration in the imagery of 'A vast canyon' suggests that ordinary supermarket shelves resembled a huge, imposing natural feature ■ the exaggeration in 'a universe of flakes, crunchies ...' compares something fairly trivial with the entirety of creation ■ 'cornucopia' suggests a bounteous profusion of beauty and riches but is used to describe the very mundane 'breakfast options' ■ the list of brand names 'Trix, Froot Loops, Chex, or Cheerios' sounds fairly childish, and is made more infantile by the addition of 'and then another over the specific variety of Cheerios' ■ 'wept bitterly ... her heart's desire' attaches high emotion to a dispute over breakfast cereal ■ mocking description of 'some sort of sawdust in teddy bear shapes and radioactive pastels' shows a contempt for the gaudy packaging and unhealthy content

Question			Expected response	Max. mark	Additional guidance
					■ the two short simple sentences 'I made an executive decision. We would go to a restaurant for breakfast' after the lengthy, list-like descriptions and high emotions are tongue-in-cheek, deliberately downbeat
					■ the lists of choices offered in the restaurant are almost ridiculously long, mocking the absurdity of the choice (and perhaps the waitress's skill in memorising them)
					■ description of the waitress's reaction ('scandalised ... dereliction of the God-given duty ... weird ... un-American') uses words usually associated with profound concepts, suggests he felt bemused at such a strong reaction
					■ list of choices in jeans store is amusingly long and detailed
					■ the question 'Relaxed, or easy?' refers to styles of jeans, but he turns it into a comment on his own state of mind: 'Neither'.
2			Candidates must use their own words. No marks for straight lifts from the passage. 2 marks may be awarded for detailed/insightful comment. 1 mark for more basic comment. (Marks may be awarded 2 or 1+1.)	2	Possible answers include: ■ they dislike/disapprove of having to make so many choices ■ in the past many of the decisions they now have to make were made for them (by government officials) ■ worrying about choice diverts time and effort away from potentially more useful pursuits ■ as intellectuals they believe that there are more important things in life than consumer choice ■ having too much choice is psychologically detrimental.
3	a)		Candidates must use their own words. No marks for straight lifts from the passage. 2 marks may be awarded for detailed/insightful comment. 1 mark for more basic comment. (Marks may be awarded 2 or 1+1.)	2	Possible answers include: ■ it wastes time ■ it inevitably leads to dissatisfaction, disillusionment, fear that we could have made a better choice ■ we are misled into believing there is a perfect, ideal choice.
	b)		For full marks there should be comments on at least two examples. 2 marks may be awarded for detailed/insightful comment plus quotation/ reference.	4	Possible answers include: ■ 'shackled' suggests we are bound, imprisoned, have no control ■ 'demands' suggests that choice imposes on us, insists we behave in a certain way ■ 'stolen' suggests that something (time) is being taken from us illegally, without our knowledge or permission

Question			Expected response	Max. mark	Additional guidance
			1 mark for more basic comment plus quotation/reference. 0 marks for quotation/reference alone. (Marks may be awarded 2+2, 2+1+1 or 1+1+1+1.)		<ul><li>'bogus and repetitive menu' suggests it is false, deceitful; that it is tedious, tiresome, monotonous</li><li>'inescapable' suggests it cannot be avoided, it is always going to happen</li><li>'quest' suggests a long, difficult, arduous search for something perhaps impossible</li><li>'hopelessly' suggests we are doomed to failure, makes us sound almost impotent</li><li>'thing' suggests a vagueness, as if we don't even know what it is we are searching for</li><li>'live in fear' suggests a lingering, permanent sense of disappointment hanging over us.</li></ul>
4			Candidates must use their own words. No marks for straight lifts from the passage. 2 marks may be awarded for detailed/insightful comment. 1 mark for more basic comment. (Marks may be awarded 2 or 1+1.)	2	Possible answers include:<ul><li>the 'maximiser' believes it is possible to find the ideal choice; the 'satisficer' accepts that this is not possible</li><li>the 'maximiser' expends time and energy trying to find the best choice; the 'satisificer' chooses quickly, accepts that the choice might not be ideal</li><li>the 'maximiser' is forever tormented that the wrong choice has been made and will never be happy; the 'satisficer' lives with his/her choice and is content.</li></ul>
5			Candidates must use their own words. No marks for straight lifts from the passage. 2 marks may be awarded for detailed/insightful comment. 1 mark for more basic comment. (Marks may be awarded 2+1 or 1+1+1.)	3	Possible answers include:<ul><li>consumer satisfaction is not in direct proportion to the number of choices available</li><li>the narrower the choice the more likely it is that a purchase will be made</li><li>even 'special offers' suffer when there is choice because consumers are unable to make the choice</li><li>decisions are often put off, delayed when there is too much choice</li><li>the false idea that there is a perfect, correct choice makes us unwilling to commit to a decision</li><li>consumers end up never being satisfied.</li></ul>
6			For full marks there must be comments on both language and ideas, but these do not have to be evenly divided, and there will be overlap. 2 marks may be awarded for detailed/insightful comment (plus quotation/reference for language points).	4	Possible answers include: **ideas:**<ul><li>introduces idea that a change might be coming – acts as a counterbalance to the problems outlined in the passage</li><li>specific examples of solutions (internet, shopping list) provide a positive way forward</li><li>offers definite advice: don't agonise over it</li><li>supports/reinforces the 'satisficer' idea from earlier</li></ul>

Question			Expected response	Max. mark	Additional guidance
			1 mark for more basic comment (plus quotation/ reference for language points). 0 marks for quotation/ reference alone. (Marks may be awarded 2+2, 2+1+1 or 1+1+1+1.)		▪ the stewardess's 'real anguish' at there being no choice recalls the idea that for some, choice is hugely important ▪ his relief at not having to make a choice supports his argument that making choices can be stressful ▪ the joke in 'We all have to make satisifices' picks up on the term from Schwartz's book. **language:** ▪ 'But' … suggests a turning point, that perhaps there is an answer ▪ 'revolution is brewing' suggests people are preparing to rise up against an unfair, evil force ▪ 'tyranny of choice' reinforces his argument that choice is an oppressive, undemocratic imposition ▪ the tongue-in-cheek explanation of 'self-binding pre-commitment' as 'This used to be known as a shopping list' mocks the social scientists' jargon and is in keeping with light-hearted tone at start ▪ the parenthetical '(i.e., just about anything)' shows his low opinion of the time spent on unnecessary choice ▪ the tone in the final line where he shows relief at not having to make a choice and makes a private joke about 'satisfices' matches the light-hearted tone at the start.

Question on both passages

Question			Expected response	Max. mark	Additional guidance
7			Candidates may use bullet points in this final question, or write a number of linked statements. Evidence from the passage may include quotations, but these should be supported by explanations. The approach to marking is shown in the 'Additional guidance' column. Key areas of agreement are shown in the grid below. Other answers are possible.	5	The mark for this question should reflect the quality of response in two areas: ■ identification of the key areas of agreement in attitude/ideas ■ the level of detail given in support. The following guidelines should be used: ■ **5 marks** – identification of three key areas of agreement with insightful use of supporting evidence ■ **4 marks** – identification of three key areas of agreement with appropriate use of supporting evidence ■ **3 marks** – identification of three key areas of agreement ■ **2 marks** – identification of two key areas of agreement ■ **1 mark** – identification of one key area of agreement ■ **0 marks** – failure to identify one key area of agreement and/or misunderstanding of task. **NB** A candidate who identifies only two key areas of agreement may be awarded up to a maximum of 4 marks, as follows: ■ 2 marks for identification of two key areas of agreement **plus either** ■ a further 1 mark for appropriate use of supporting evidence to a total of 3 marks **or** ■ a further 2 marks for detailed/insightful use of supporting evidence to a total of 4 marks. A candidate who identifies only one key area of agreement may be awarded up to a maximum of 2 marks, as follows: ■ 1 mark for identification of one key area of agreement ■ a further 1 mark for use of supporting evidence to a total of 2 marks.

	Area of agreement	Passage 1	Passage 2
1	the extent of choice	too much of it everywhere; it pervades many areas of modern life	is embedded in consumer choice, in financial matters, in personal affairs
2	principal problem	it dominates us, weighs us down, is 'tyrannical'	it is 'oppressive'
3	psychological impact	causes mental strain, family arguments, loss of control	causes depression, mental 'paralysis'
4	effect on decision-making	makes confident decision-making almost impossible; leads to fear/worry that wrong decision has been made	leads to a lingering concern that wrong choice has been made, 'the burden of choice'; the perfect choice is illusory
5	the role of business/commerce	it is driven by/is a tool of modern business methods and advertising	modern business employs complexity of choice as a method of diverting attention from competition; sense that consumers are being cheated, tricked
6	response to Schwartz's book	sympathises with the 'satisificer' over the 'maximiser', who is 'doomed ...'	condemns 'maximisers', who are 'never happy'; supports 'satisificers'
7	suggested solution	don't agonise over choice, make an early decision and live with it	don't even try for 'the best'; accept what 'will do'

Paper 2: Critical Reading

Section 1 – Scottish Text – 20 marks

NB The final question (for 10 marks) on each text should be marked using the general instructions below. Text-specific guidance for each final question is given at the relevant point.

Up to 2 marks can be achieved for identifying elements of commonality as identified in the question.

A further 2 marks can be achieved for reference to the extract given.

6 additional marks can be achieved for discussion of similar references to at least one other part of the text (or to another short story or poem by the writer).

In practice this means:

- 2 marks for identification of **commonality**, e.g. theme, characterisation, use of imagery, setting, or any other key element.

From the **extract**:

- 2 marks for detailed/insightful comment plus quotation/reference
- 1 mark for more basic comment plus quotation/reference
- 0 marks for quotation/reference alone

From at least one **other part of the text** (or one other poem or short story):

- as above for up to 6 marks.

Text 1 – Drama – *The Slab Boys* by John Byrne

Question	Expected response	Max. mark	Additional guidance
1	2 marks may be awarded for detailed/insightful comment plus quotation/reference. 1 mark for more basic comment plus quotation/reference. 0 marks for quotation/reference alone. (Marks may be awarded 1+1.)	2	Possible answers include: Character: ■ brash, self-confident, menacing/bullying/aggressive/threatening Reference to and explanation of: ■ self-confident, laying down the law – 'Burton's Corner … quarter to … okay?' ■ brash, less than diplomatic – 'put some cream on that pimple … I swear it's twice the size it was this morning' ■ openly insulting – 'look at him … he's a skelf' ■ rude, aggressive – 'Aw, go to hell' ■ relishes the possibility of Phil's suffering – 'He eats smouts like you for his breakfast' ■ bullying, menacing – 'If you're not there on the dot …' ■ threatening – 'so be warned!'
2	2 marks may be awarded for detailed/insightful comment plus quotation/reference. 1 mark for more basic comment plus quotation/reference. 0 marks for quotation/reference alone. (Marks may be awarded 2+2, 2+1+1 or 1+1+1+1.)	4	Possible answers include: ■ he speaks *'Bravely'*, suggesting he is prepared to stand up for himself ■ he is not interested in any apology/explanation from Alan ■ unconcerned tone of 'Well, you guys …' suggests confidence ■ he is not embarrassed/ashamed/shy to say he is getting a lift from the boss ■ the dismissive 'keep that fitch' suggests he's moved on to better things ■ he keeps the money – doesn't give in to Spanky's demand ■ he has the confidence to come back in ■ he issues orders to Spanky – puts him in his place ■ he uses Spanky's surname to sound controlling, dominant ■ he is cheeky to Phil about his laziness ■ he restores the pen to its rightful owner.

Question			Expected response	Max. mark	Additional guidance
3			2 marks may be awarded for detailed/insightful comment plus quotation/reference. 1 mark for more basic comment plus quotation/reference. 0 marks for quotation/reference alone. (Marks may be awarded 2+2, 2+1+1 or 1+1+1+1.)	4	Possible answers include: ■ he sneers at Phil's self-pity ('doing a pretty good job of that on your own') ■ the mock geniality of 'buy you a small beer perhaps' ■ his use of 'Sparky' – pay-back for all the wrong names he's been called ■ the reference to stepping on fingers portrays him as Neanderthal ■ 'cabinet's an embarrassment' – repeating Curry's earlier words aligns Alan with the bosses, superior to Phil and Spanky.
4			Candidates can answer in bullet points in this final question, or write a number of linked statements. Marks for this question should be allocated following the guidelines given at the start of these Marking Instructions. See page 132.	10	Possible references include: Lucille: ■ the complications over who is to be her date at the Staffie form an important driver of the plot ■ she represents a strong, independent, self-confident female perhaps not typical of the period ■ her amusing turns of phrase and her sharp-tongued ability to stand up to Phil add to the humour of the play ■ her being terrified by the appearance of Hector at the window provides one of the highlights of the dramatic action. Hector: ■ as the hapless butt of Phil and Spanky's mockery, he is vital to the comedy of the play ■ the references to his mother's suicide contribute to the darker side of the play and its exploration of mental health ■ the farcical nature of his make-over is a key element of the slapstick humour in the play ■ his changed status by the end of the play (getting a desk) is an ironic twist, and contradicts much of what Phil believes and complains about.

Text 2 – Drama – *The Cheviot, the Stag and the Black, Black Oil* by John McGrath

Question		Expected response	Max. mark	Additional guidance
5	a)	2 marks may be awarded for detailed/ insightful comment plus quotation/reference. 1 mark for more basic comment plus quotation/reference. 0 marks for quotation/ reference alone. (Marks may be awarded 1+1.)	2	Possible answers include: <ul><li>spiv, on the make, self-seeking – the seemingly endless list of tacky money-making schemes he can reel off</li><li>cynical, corrupt – 'these are the best men money can buy'</li><li>obsessed with modernity – 'the thing of the future', 'to cater for the younger set'</li><li>no sense of traditional beauty, values – 'formerly there was hee-haw but scenery'</li><li>slovenly of speech – 'yous … wes've … and that … hee-haw'.</li></ul>
	b)	2 marks may be awarded for detailed/ insightful comment plus quotation/reference. 1 mark for more basic comment plus quotation/reference. 0 marks for quotation/ reference alone. (Marks may be awarded 2+2, 2+1+1 or 1+1+1+1.)	4	Possible answers include: <ul><li>'Crammem Inn': 'Inn' suggests something welcoming, traditional, but this has idea of cramming in as many as possible, unscrupulous overcrowding</li><li>'High Rise Motorcroft': 'croft' suggests traditional, homely, but Motorcroft sounds industrial, lots of cars, etc.; also anything high rise would look out of place</li><li>'Frying Scotsman' is a pun on Flying Scotsman (an object of pride, beauty); changing to 'Frying' is a dig at Scots' penchant for fried food</li><li>'All Night Chipperama' – hint of 'panorama', suggesting scenic view, but 'Chipperama' suggests on a lavish, garish scale, associated with unhealthy food; 'all night' would be noisy, disruptive</li><li>'Fingal's Caff' – pun on Fingal's Cave – romantic, historical; 'caff' (as opposed to 'café') has overtones of cheap and nasty</li><li>'seaweed-suppers-in-the-basket' – 'supper' idea is joke from 'fish supper' etc.; 'in-the-basket' is a dig at the then current fashion for meals such as chicken-in-the-basket</li><li>'draught Drambuie' – having a powerful liqueur on draught is ludicrous, suggests he either doesn't know what it is or sees no problem in drinking spirits by the pint</li><li>'Grouse-a-go-go' – some kind of discotheque, coined with the 'a-go-go' tag from current fashion with something/anything remotely Highland</li><li>'a drive-in clachan on every hill-top' – 'clachan' suggests something old, established, with a sense of community; 'drive-in' is the ultimate in modern convenience.</li></ul>

Question			Expected response	Max. mark	Additional guidance
6			2 marks may be awarded for detailed/ insightful comment plus quotation/reference. 1 mark for more basic comment plus quotation/reference. 0 marks for quotation/ reference alone. (Marks may be awarded 2+2, 2+1+1 or 1+1+1+1.)	4	Possible answers include: ■ his very name: Vat of Glenlivet – meant to sound like a traditional Highland title, but in fact is a joke about whisky and overindulgence ■ 'these are my mountains' – ridiculous claim, as if he glibly believes he owns the landscape (+ humorous hint of song of same title) ■ 'ancient Scotch family' – use of 'Scotch' ironically shows he is anglified, out of touch ■ 'I represent the true spirit of the Highlands' – vain, pompous (although perhaps, in an ironic way, true) ■ 'hordes of common people' – shows his unquestioning contempt for 'common people', comically condemned out of his own mouth ■ 'No amount of money could' – we rather suspect this won't be true ■ 'the couthie way of life' – cringe-making reference to imaginary lifestyle ■ confusion of Bantu and Highlander, sherpa and stalker shows he doesn't even know which continent he's in ■ approves of Highlanders only because they're good servants ■ 'ghillie-wallah' – again confusing Indian servant with Highland one ■ unconscious double entendre in 'doing up your flies' ■ 'wouldn't part [for] half a million' – yet quickly begins a bartering session which is soon settled ■ 'Cash'/'Done': comic conclusion, like a rehearsed routine.
7			Candidates can answer in bullet points in this final question, or write a number of linked statements. Marks for this question should be allocated following the guidelines given at the start of these Marking Instructions. See page 132.	10	Possible references include: ■ Andy McChuckemup: corrupt businessman willing to degrade anything for profit ■ Lord Vat: the easily-bought landowner ■ the Minister: blames Highlanders for their own misfortunes; full of apocalyptic warnings; connives with the landlords ■ the judge: blatant bias in favour of Sellar ■ Harriet Beecher Stowe: sees Countess of Sutherland as 'enlightened, charming lady' ■ Lord Selkirk: self-interested exploitation of Highlanders abroad ■ Lord Crask and Lady Phosphate: use Highlands as their personal playground, show crass ignorance of Highlands ■ the Duke of Sutherland's recruiting speech ■ Texas Jim: with his square dance and love of his 'home' ■ the characters represented by the two Singers (Dr Green of Surrey, Herr Heinrich Harr, etc.).

Text 3 – Drama – *Men Should Weep* by Ena Lamont Stewart

Question			Expected response	Max. mark	Additional guidance
8	a)		2 marks may be awarded for detailed/insightful comment plus quotation/reference. 1 mark for more basic comment plus quotation/reference. 0 marks for quotation/reference alone. (Marks may be awarded 2+2, 2+1+1 or 1+1+1+1.)	4	Possible answers include: ■ defensive of her role: 'Ye canna help …', 'I dae the best I can' ■ defensive of her family: 'You leave John alane', 'He does his best for us' ■ sentimental: 'I still love John. And whit's more, he loves me' ■ self-deluding: 'Aye! I'm happy!', 'I'm sorry for you, Lily.'
	b)		2 marks may be awarded for detailed/insightful comment plus quotation/reference. 1 mark for more basic comment plus quotation/reference. 0 marks for quotation/reference alone. (Marks may be awarded 1+1.)	2	Possible answers include: ■ she speaks her mind, not afraid to be negative: 'midden', 'No much o a best', 'nae' repeated ■ quick to placate, conciliate: 'O.K. O.K. …' ■ sense of humour: 'photies to the Sunday papers … Is this a record?'
9			2 marks may be awarded for detailed/insightful comment plus quotation/reference. 1 mark for more basic comment plus quotation/reference. 0 marks for quotation/reference alone. (Marks may be awarded 2+2, 2+1+1 or 1+1+1+1.)	4	Possible answers include: ■ the key ideas are: the back and forth, tennis-match-style, balanced nature of the exchanges, and the way each pair of lines is linked to the next by a word or an idea, e.g.: 　■ balance: 'Servin …' – 'Livin …'; 'in a Coocaddens pub' – 'in a slum'; 'brutes o men' – 'a useless man' 　■ link: 'weans' 　■ balance: 'his greetin weans' – 'They're *my* weans!' 　■ link: 'workin … work' 　■ balance: '*paid* for my work' – 'paid wi love' 　■ link: 'airms roon ye/me' 　■ balance 'a man's …' – '*Men*!' 　■ link: 'They're a dirty beasts' – 'a lumped thegither' 　■ balance: 'Ye're daft!' – 'You're *saft*!'

Question			Expected response	Max. mark	Additional guidance
10			Candidates can answer in bullet points in this final question, or write a number of linked statements. Marks for this question should be allocated following the guidelines given at the start of these Marking Instructions. See page 132.	10	Possible references include: ■ John's less than convincing efforts to support his family ■ John's refusal to visit Bertie, inability to come to terms with Bertie's illness ■ John's inability to cope with Jenny in any of their major confrontations ■ John's passivity in general and especially at the end where he is physically drained and unable to respond ■ Alec's laziness, slovenly habits, and occasional resorting to violence when unable to express his feelings ■ Alec's rather pathetic reliance on his mother ■ Alec's submissiveness to Isa ■ Alec's inability to cope with Isa's infidelity and desertion.

Text 1 – Prose – *The Crater* by Iain Crichton Smith

Question			Expected response	Max. mark	Additional guidance
11			2 marks may be awarded for detailed/insightful comment plus quotation/reference. 1 mark for more basic comment plus quotation/reference. 0 marks for quotation/reference alone. (Marks may be awarded 2+2, 2+1+1 or 1+1+1+1.)	4	Possible answers include: ■ 'screamed' suggests uncontrolled, panicky, high-pitched, in pain ■ 'bubbling' suggests feeble, dislocated, connotations of something vaguely supernatural, unworldly ■ 'splashing' suggests frantic activity ■ 'breathing, frantic breathing' suggests someone struggling to stay alive ■ 'splashings came closer' suggests something menacing getting nearer ■ 'voice was like an animal's' suggests inhuman, lack of control ■ 'a mixture of curses and prayers' – a surreal, confused combination of anger and invocation.

Question			Expected response	Max. mark	Additional guidance
12			2 marks may be awarded for detailed/insightful comment plus quotation/reference. 1 mark for more basic comment plus quotation/reference. 0 marks for quotation/reference alone. (Marks may be awarded 2+2, 2+1+1 or 1+1+1+1.)	4	Possible answers include: ■ 'as if there was a great fish at the end of a line' suggests that he's struggling with some mythical creature ■ 'He felt it moving' – short sentence creates feeling of shock, threat ■ 'moon shone suddenly out' – abrupt, dramatic change in light ■ 'in that moment he saw it' – sudden revelation; use of unspecific 'it' reinforces dreamlike effect ■ 'covered with greenish slime' – sickening, disgusting ■ 'an obscene mermaid' – something usually considered attractive and glamorous is distorted ■ 'two eyes, white in the green face' – disembodied, unsettling ■ 'the mouth, gritted, tried not to let the blood through' – suggests the effort, the pain, the suffering ■ 'monster of the deep' suggests a frightening, threatening, aggressive being from another world ■ 'he said to the monster below' – idea of dialogue with a 'monster' is disturbing ■ 'emerging from the deep' – suggestion of approaching threat, some sort of prehistoric monster rising from a swamp ■ 'all green, all mottled, like a disease' – horrific description of a slimy, blotchy creature, which is likened to a sickness/virus ■ 'stench' – emphasises the overwhelming unpleasantness and horror of the scene ■ 'It hung there ...' – creates a picture of something supernatural, defying gravity.
13			2 marks may be awarded for detailed/insightful comment plus quotation/reference. 1 mark for more basic comment plus quotation/reference. 0 marks for quotation/reference alone. (Marks may be awarded 1+1.)	2	Possible answers include: ■ it creates a sense of the cruelty of nature, the moon as observer of the macabre proceedings below ■ it is as if, while Robert frantically (and heroically) seeks to rescue his comrade, a greater power knows the futility of it ■ it prepares the reader for the shattering of Robert's elation at his 'rescue'.

Question			Expected response	Max. mark	Additional guidance
14			Candidates can answer in bullet points in this final question, or write a number of linked statements. Marks for this question should be allocated following the guidelines given at the start of these Marking Instructions. See page 132.	10	Possible references include: ■ *The Crater* – tension among the men during the raid; tension as they wait to see if the soldier can be rescued ■ *The Telegram* – tension between the two women (their backgrounds, their sons' status); tension as elder approaches ■ *In Church* – tension as Colin enters the church, as he listens to the increasingly frenzied sermon ■ *The Painter* – tension during the fight ■ *The Red Door* – tension as Murdo discovers the mysterious painting of the door; tension as he sets out for Mary's house ■ *Mother and Son* – tension as animosity between mother and son builds up to climax; tension in the uncertainty of the ending.

Text 2 – Prose – *The Bright Spade* by George Mackay Brown

Question			Expected response	Max. mark	Additional guidance
15			2 marks may be awarded for detailed/insightful comment plus quotation/ reference. 1 mark for more basic comment plus quotation/ reference. 0 marks for quotation/ reference alone. (Marks may be awarded 2+2, 2+1+1 or 1+1+1+1.)	4	Possible answers include: ■ the preponderance of simple, flat, sentences ■ the absence of any elaboration ■ the use of simple reportage, statement of fact ■ the absence of comment, reflection – even at a detail as gruesome as the dog gnawing the corpse or a detail as bizarre as Jacob's acceptance of the fiddle ■ even the imagery ('shell ... chrysalis') sounds more factual than evocative.
16			2 marks may be awarded for detailed/insightful comment plus quotation/ reference. 1 mark for more basic comment plus quotation/ reference. 0 marks for quotation/ reference alone. (Marks may be awarded 1+1.)	2	Possible answers include: ■ seems to be looked up to, respected – speaks uninterrupted, his plan is accepted without demur ■ unemotional, absence of self-pity when he describes what he has eaten ■ realistic, practical, pragmatic plan ■ includes himself in risky venture – brave, prepared to accept risks on behalf of others, sacrifice for the community.

Question			Expected response	Max. mark	Additional guidance
17			2 marks may be awarded for detailed/insightful comment plus quotation/reference. 1 mark for more basic comment plus quotation/reference. 0 marks for quotation/reference alone. (Marks may be awarded 2+2, 2+1+1 or 1+1+1+1.)	**4**	Possible answers include: ■ aware that he is benefitting from others' suffering ('I have done better this winter than anyone') ■ makes (minor) concession by not accepting payment for the seven men … ■ … but reverts to usual collection of something/anything ('set of Nantucket harpoons') ■ perhaps some sense of guilt ('God grant …') … ■ … but more likely a simple acceptance ■ deeply rooted in cycle of the seasons, knows that winter and death will come round again ■ accepts his role in the community with a sense of resignation.
18			Candidates can answer in bullet points in this final question, or write a number of linked statements. Marks for this question should be allocated following the guidelines given at the start of these Marking Instructions. See page 132.	**10**	Possible references include: ■ *The Bright Spade* – the brightness of the spade itself; the various 'payments' made to Jacob ■ *Tartan* – the tartan cloth; the axes; the soup; the ale; Olaf's poem ■ *A Time To Keep* – frequent references to fire and light; the twelve sections (calendar months); the new shoes; the harvest ■ *The Whaler's Return* – the allegorical nature of Flaws' journey; the 'tinkers' wedding', money, alcohol ■ *The Wireless Set* – the set itself; the telegram; the eggs and the crabs ■ *The Eye of the Hurricane* – the wreck of the Danish ship; the Captain's rum; Barclay's book and his writer's block; the twelve Salvationists.

Text 3 – Prose – *The Trick Is To Keep Breathing* by Janice Galloway

Question			Expected response	Max. mark	Additional guidance
19			2 marks may be awarded for detailed/insightful comment plus quotation/ reference. 1 mark for more basic comment plus quotation/ reference. 0 marks for quotation/ reference alone. (Marks may be awarded 1+1.)	2	Possible answers include: ■ the doctor's lateness suggests a lack of care ■ 'sea-coloured corridor' – the sea has unpleasant associations for Joy ■ 'no pictures and all the curtains closed' suggests cold, dark, claustrophobic, inhospitable ■ 'smells like dog in the rain' suggests pungent, non-human, sickening ■ the absence of any preliminary chat suggests a very functional, bureaucratic approach ■ 'Well?' suggests a very abrupt, uncaring tone ■ 'horrible jacket' suggests even his clothing is off-putting.
20			2 marks may be awarded for detailed/insightful comment plus quotation/ reference. 1 mark for more basic comment plus quotation/ reference. 0 marks for quotation/ reference alone. (Marks may be awarded 2+2, 2+1+1 or 1+1+1+1.)	4	Possible answers include: ■ the profusion of short questions is indicative of limited interaction between speakers ■ the 'stage directions' about Patient being 'Mesmerised', 'Confused', not able to speak, tears welling give a general picture of her discomfort and inability to communicate well ■ 'Well what?' – her response to Dr's opening shows she's doesn't understand ■ 'I thought you would start' – shows she doesn't know what's going on ■ 'Start what?' – Dr is (deliberately?) showing he doesn't want to engage ■ 'Yes. So what ...' – a very perfunctory response to Patient's statement ■ 'I want to know ...' – 'I don't know ...' – total breakdown of communication ■ 'So.' – as if it has all been explained, nothing further to say ■ 'Any other questions?' – with a hint that they will be dismissed as quickly as the first ■ 'How long have you been here did you say?' – she has already told him.

Question			Expected response	Max. mark	Additional guidance
21			2 marks may be awarded for detailed/insightful comment plus quotation/reference. 1 mark for more basic comment plus quotation/reference. 0 marks for quotation/reference alone. (Marks may be awarded 2+2, 2+1+1 or 1+1+1+1.)	**4**	Possible answers include: <ul><li>'Sighing' suggests impatience, as if dealing with a stupid child</li><li>'I suppose' – as if he's having to do the thinking for her</li><li>'To go home for the weekend?' – questioning intonation as if explaining something very simple to someone not very bright</li><li>'... all right?' – patronising tone</li><li>'I don't know what that's supposed to mean' – unhelpful reply to someone obviously distressed</li><li>'Take your time. [Silence] Right then' – invites her to take her time and then doesn't give her any</li><li>... taps the bundle of papers ... folds his arms' – making his impatience obvious</li><li>'The interview is over' – very abrupt.</li></ul>
22			Candidates can answer in bullet points in this final question, or write a number of linked statements. Marks for this question should be allocated following the guidelines given at the start of these Marking Instructions. See page 132.	**10**	Possible references include: <ul><li>overall impression of a bureaucratic, uncaring system</li><li>Doctor Three: gives impression of not caring; often rude and/or indifferent</li><li>the Health Visitor is ineffectual and offers bland advice</li><li>Doctor One asks stupid questions and makes her very uncomfortable</li><li>Doctor Two repeats questions, offers little help (though does make some effort)</li><li>Tom at Ward Meeting is well-meaning but ineffectual</li><li>many pointless rather childish activities (e.g. Occupational Therapy)</li><li>various minor characters (Moira, Ben ...) basically decent people but can achieve little in a regimented system.</li></ul>

Text 4 – Prose – *Sunset Song* by Lewis Grassic Gibbon

Question			Expected response	Max. mark	Additional guidance
23			2 marks may be awarded for detailed/insightful comment plus quotation/reference. 1 mark for more basic comment plus quotation/reference. 0 marks for quotation/reference alone. (Marks may be awarded 2+2, 2+1+1 or 1+1+1+1.)	4	Possible answers include: ■ 'marched out' suggests an element of pomposity ■ 'this class or that' suggests little interest in the class, any old one will do ■ 'Right fond …' suggests a good awareness of his social climbing, deference ■ structure of 'if … and … and …' almost suggests he has careful, logical plan of whom to prefer ■ 'stroke your arm' suggests an unhealthy interest in the pupil ■ 'slow sing-song' suggests affectation, dishonesty ■ the representation of his extended vowel sounds ('Nooooooooooooo') etc. is exaggerated for comic effect ■ the representation of his actual vowel sounds ('*quate raight*') makes him sound pretentious, false ■ 'flute' suggests unnatural, high-pitched, affected ■ comparing the drawing to a 'pig' (dirty, not known for beauty) shows he is prepared to be downright offensive.
24			2 marks may be awarded for detailed/insightful comment plus quotation/reference. 1 mark for more basic comment plus quotation/reference. 0 marks for quotation/reference alone. (Marks may be awarded 2+2, 2+1+1 or 1+1+1+1.)	4	Possible answers include: ■ their social climbing, fondness for those higher in society ■ their hypocrisy – despite their own humble origins, they despise children from poor backgrounds and they align themselves with the 'gentry' ■ their patronising treatment of her because of her origins ■ their unequal treatment of pupils – unjustified praise of 'the Fordyce girl' (more to do with her father's money) ■ they openly embarrass Chris (reference to her father's pigs; reading out her essay) ■ (Murgetson) poor discipline, capacity for unrestrained anger, verging on violence – yet succumbs pathetically to the 'simpering' of the French teacher.
25			2 marks may be awarded for detailed/insightful comment plus quotation/reference. 1 mark for more basic comment plus quotation/reference. 0 marks for quotation/reference alone. (Marks may be awarded 1+1.)	2	Possible answers include: ■ listing structure 'and … and … and' suggests the many things she misses ■ appeal to senses – sound ('champ of horses') ■ appeal to senses – smell ('dung') ■ appeal to senses – sight ('brown, grained') ■ 'sick (to be home)' suggests intensity of desire.

Question			Expected response	Max. mark	Additional guidance
26			Candidates can answer in bullet points in this final question, or write a number of linked statements. Marks for this question should be allocated following the guidelines given at the start of these Marking Instructions. See page 132.	10	Possible references include: ■ her decision to reject the 'English Chris' and to work on the land ■ she does as she thinks fit and proper, prepared to go against convention (e.g. attendance at father's funeral, not influenced by lawyer's doubts about her taking on the farm) ■ she copes with/survives desertion and loss (mother's suicide, Marget's leaving, Will's emigration, father's death, loss of Ewan, Long Rob, Chae) ■ her healthy, 'modern' attitude to sex, no shame at contemplation of her own body ■ her reluctance to condemn outright (e.g. the teachers at Duncairn, her treatment by father and by Will) ■ her love of education (especially the 'magic land' of books) and her sensitive, poetic, intellectual side – which can set her apart from Ewan, despite her love for him.

Text 5 – Prose – *The Cone-Gatherers* by Robin Jenkins

Question	Expected response	Max. mark	Additional guidance
27	2 marks may be awarded for detailed/insightful comment plus quotation/ reference. 1 mark for more basic comment plus quotation/ reference. 0 marks for quotation/ reference alone. (Marks may be awarded 1+1.)	2	Possible answers include: ■ 'feebleminded' suggests he sees him as stupid, subnormal ■ 'hunchback' – a very belittling, offensive word, suggests he focuses on the deformity ■ 'grovelling' distorts Calum's attempts at mercy into something demeaning, as if he's begging, bowing and scraping ■ 'obscene' suggests any sound from Calum would be seen as something disgusting, lascivious.

28	2 marks may be awarded for detailed/insightful comment plus quotation/ reference.
	1 mark for more basic comment plus quotation/ reference.
	0 marks for quotation/ reference alone.
	(Marks may be awarded 2+2, 2+1+1 or 1+1+1+1.)
		4	Possible answers include:
			■ that he had 'waited over an hour' just to see them suggests it is an obsession
			■ 'purgatory of humiliation' is an exaggerated way to describe his feelings, suggests how deeply affected he is
			■ 'as if … forced to wait upon them as upon his masters' – a reversal of the norm, suggests how distorted his view is
			■ his apparent desire to see the cone-gatherers come to harm, a sense of relish in 'come crashing down' and 'lie dead on the ground'
			■ the extended metaphor in which he imagines himself standing on floor of sea and sees features around him as if they were underwater – bizarre, dreamlike, surreal:
			  ■ 'standing on the floor of a fantastic sea' – acknowledges that it's dreamlike, fanciful
			  ■ 'with an owl and a herd of roe-deer flitting by quiet as fish' – terrestrial creatures are transformed in his mind into aquatic ones
			  ■ 'ferns and bronzen brackens … gleamed like seaweed' – terrestrial flora are transformed into aquatic ones, ironically described in terms of great beauty
			  ■ 'spruce trees … like submarine monsters' – distorted view of trees as dangerous/ threatening underwater beasts.

Question			Expected response	Max. mark	Additional guidance
29			2 marks may be awarded for detailed/insightful comment plus quotation/reference. 1 mark for more basic comment plus quotation/reference. 0 marks for quotation/reference alone. (Marks may be awarded 2+2, 2+1+1 or 1+1+1+1.)	4	Possible answers include: ■ 'the overspreading tree of revulsion in him' – recognises the hatred within him as organic, taking him over totally ■ 'his stronghold and sanctuary' gives the idea of him being at war, needing to defend himself, being isolated ■ 'fortify his sanity and hope' shows awareness that he is mentally unstable and wishes to fight against this ■ 'invaded and defiled' depicts the cone-gatherers as an enemy, a threat, corrupting, dirty ■ 'its cleansing and reviving virtues' depicts the wood as a place of healing, suggests he views nature as perhaps more powerful than human agency ■ 'like the whining prostrations of a heathen in front of an idol' – he sees Calum as something alien, primitive, submissive, lacking dignity, entirely different ■ 'diabolical joke' – as if dreamed up by the devil, intended to cause him (Duror) suffering; 'joke' because of the incongruity of the ugly features and the beautiful face.
30			Candidates can answer in bullet points in this final question, or write a number of linked statements. Marks for this question should be allocated following the guidelines given at the start of these Marking Instructions. See page 132.	10	Possible references include: ■ the general idea of the eternal struggle of Good and Evil, Innocence and Worldliness ■ Duror's irrational dislike of the cone-gatherers from the moment of their arrival ■ the different attitudes to wildlife (the injured rabbit) ■ Duror's support for the Nazis' treatment of handicapped people ■ Duror's manipulation of Lady Runcie-Campbell to enlist the cone-gatherers in the deer drive ■ Duror's lying about Calum exposing himself ■ the deaths at the end – Calum as Christ, Duror as Judas/devil.

Text 1 – Poetry – *To a Mouse* by Robert Burns

Question			Expected response	Max. mark	Additional guidance
31			2 marks may be awarded for detailed/insightful comment plus quotation/reference. 1 mark for more basic comment plus quotation/reference. 0 marks for quotation/reference alone. (Marks may be awarded 1+1.)	2	Possible answers include: ■ word choice of 'wee-bit housie' suggests something modest, basic, unelaborate ■ the minor sentence/exclamation suggests the poet feels shocked at the loss ■ word choice of 'silly' suggests something very simple, basic ■ word choice of 'strewin' suggests the relentless destruction caused by the wind ■ alliteration of 'naethin, now' slightly emphasises the mouse's plight ■ word choice of 'bleak December' suggests the depressing, austere situation at the height of winter ■ word choice of 'Baith snell an' keen!' suggests the unpleasantness and suffering the mouse will face.

32			2 marks may be awarded for detailed/insightful comment plus quotation/reference.
			1 mark for more basic comment plus quotation/reference.
			0 marks for quotation/reference alone.
			(Marks may be awarded 2+2, 2+1+1 or 1+1+1+1.)
				4	Possible answers include:
					■ the mouse's way of life:
					  ■ 'Thou saw … Thou thought' suggesting planning
					  ■ contrast of 'bare an' waste' and 'cozie' to suggest what mouse was trying to guard against
					  ■ 'dwell' suggests the safety, protection the mouse had hoped for
					■ 'cost thee mony a weary nibble' – emphasises the effort that has been expended on the nest
					■ man's destruction of his plans:
					  ■ 'crash!' – onomatopoeic representation of the sudden destruction
					  ■ 'thou's turn'd out' – idea of him being rejected
					  ■ 'cruel coulter' – alliteration emphasises the harshness of the plough
					  ■ 'cranreuch cauld' – alliteration emphasises the harshness of the weather he will face as a result of man's interference.

Question			Expected response	Max. mark	Additional guidance
33			2 marks may be awarded for detailed/insightful comment plus quotation/reference. 1 mark for more basic comment plus quotation/reference. 0 marks for quotation/reference alone. (Marks may be awarded 2+2, 2+1+1 or 1+1+1+1.)	4	Possible answers include: ■ 'But Mousie' – the 'but' suggests moving on from the bleak picture painted in preceding lines ■ 'thou art no thy lane' – offers some sympathy, fellow feeling that others suffer ■ 'the best-laid schemes' – no matter how well planned things are ■ 'o' mice an' men' – links man and beast, shows this happens to all ■ 'aft' – it is a frequent occurrence ■ 'grief an' pain' – very pessimistic picture of suffering ■ 'For promis'd joy!' – reminds us of the hopes, the expectations we once had ■ 'Still' – concedes that mouse has one advantage ■ 'thou art blest, compar'd wi' me' – self-pity? ■ 'But och!' – tone of frustration perhaps ■ 'I guess an' fear!' finishes on an enigmatic note, but pessimism seems to dominate.
34			Candidates can answer in bullet points in this final question, or write a number of linked statements. Marks for this question should be allocated following the guidelines given at the start of these Marking Instructions. See page 132.	10	Possible references include: ■ aspects of the Standard Habbie in *To a Mouse*, *Holy Willie's Prayer*, *Address to the Deil*, *A Poet's Welcome* …: e.g. the ability to make an initial statement or observation in the first three lines and then introduce something different with the change of pace in the two short lines, often adding ironic, caustic or humorous comment; allows the poet to add a touch of drama at the climax of each stanza ■ aspects of traditional song-and-chorus structure in *A Man's a Man for a' That*: e.g. adds a sense of musicality; the repetition adds weight, confidence and commitment to the 'message'; the predictability of the rhyming suggests unshakeable belief in the sentiments; choric nature invites involvement, a sense of communal belief in the aim of brotherhood ■ tetrameter rhyming couplets in *Tam o' Shanter*: e.g. simple narrative verse form ideally suited to the context of a tavern yarn; predictable and straightforward; adaptable for fast-moving sections and slower, more contemplative passages.

Text 2 – Poetry – *Anne Hathaway* by Carol Ann Duffy

Question			Expected response	Max. mark	Additional guidance
35			2 marks may be awarded for detailed/insightful comment plus quotation/reference. 1 mark for more basic comment plus quotation/reference. 0 marks for quotation/reference alone. (Marks may be awarded 1+1.)	2	Possible answers include: ■ 'a spinning world …' suggests lively, exhilarating, breathless ■ 'forests, castles, torchlight, clifftops' (collectively or singly) suggests romantic, exotic, thrilling, dangerous ■ 'seas/where he would dive for pearls' suggests both depth and thrilling activities with potential for wealth ■ list ('forests, castles, torchlight, clifftops, seas') suggests a vast range of different things, as if she is reeling them off with pleasure.
36			2 marks may be awarded for detailed/insightful comment plus quotation/reference. 1 mark for more basic comment plus quotation/reference. 0 marks for quotation/reference alone. (Marks may be awarded 2+2, 2+1+1 or 1+1+1+1.)	4	Possible answers include: ■ The general idea is about the blurring of the distinction between life and art, that Anne sees their love as being as vital, exciting, as fulfilling as her husband's work; this idea should be developed by specific references such as: ■ 'words/were shooting stars' could possibly refer to written words, hence suggesting she sees them as exciting, romantic ■ 'my body now a softer rhyme' creates a sense of their being joined together, of belonging together (Duffy is also touching on the idea of masculine and feminine rhyme) ■ 'now echo, assonance' continues the idea of things being joined together in a pleasing way (imitated by the string of words linked by assonance: 'on', 'body', 'softer', 'to', 'echo', 'assonance', 'touch' and 'noun') ■ 'a verb dancing in the centre of a noun' suggests joyous action, sexually suggestive; hints at Shakespeare's fondness for creating verbs from nouns and therefore suggests energy, freshness in their lovemaking ■ 'I dreamed he'd written me' suggests how her love has sparked her imagination, she loves him so much that she dreams of being one of his creations ■ 'the bed/a page' continues the conflation of his creativity and their lovemaking; almost punning on idea of sheets of paper/sheets on a bed; his creativity on paper is matched by his creativity in bed ■ 'Romance/and drama played' elevates their love to a full theatrical production; as if they are acting out a dramatic (and poetic) script.

Question			Expected response	Max. mark	Additional guidance
37			2 marks may be awarded for detailed/insightful comment plus quotation/reference. 1 mark for more basic comment plus quotation/reference. 0 marks for quotation/reference alone. (Marks may be awarded 2+2, 2+1+1 or 1+1+1+1.)	4	Possible answers include: ■ the contrast between the exuberant love of Anne and her lover and the dullness of the guests, seen in 'dozed', which suggests they are inactive, and in 'dribbling their prose', a disdainful reference to the difference between the everyday nature of 'prose' and the excitement, energy of poetry ■ the vitality suggested in 'living laughing love' – emphasised by the alliteration, the smooth, liquid sound of the repeated 'l' (which contrasts with the harsher sounds of 'dozed', 'dribbling' and 'prose') ■ the dash leads into the conclusion, a dramatic separation of the descriptions of her husband alive and the acknowledgement that he lives on in her imagination ■ the consonance in 'hold' and 'held' recalls that the lovers rhymed with each other ■ the imagery of 'casket' suggests that like a strongbox for valuables her memories are precious ■ the final rhyming couplet (in imitation of the Shakespearean sonnet) brings the poem to a pleasing aural conclusion.
38			Candidates can answer in bullet points in this final question, or write a number of linked statements. Marks for this question should be allocated following the guidelines given at the start of these Marking Instructions. See page 132.	10	Possible references include: ■ *Anne Hathaway* – explores an all-encompassing, deeply physical relationship; seen in terms of exotic, romantic places and literary/artistic metaphors; contrasts the dull, unimaginative love of some with the warmth and passion of the speaker and her lover ■ *Mrs Midas* – explores the disruption of a once stable relationship, brought about by husband's greed and selfishness; explores the effect of money on romance ■ *Valentine* – explores the idea that conventional tokens of love are ineffective and that love is something dangerous, to be feared, but to be embraced ■ *Havisham* – explores the effects of rejection; the conflicting passions of the speaker (love and hate); passion begets violence ■ *Originally* – explores how attachment to place and/or culture can be altered by circumstances ■ *War Photographer* – explores a generally loveless world of areas ravaged by war contrasted with the comfortable complacency of 'Rural England'.

Text 3 – Poetry – *Last Supper* by Liz Lochhead

Question			Expected response	Max. mark	Additional guidance
39			2 marks may be awarded for detailed/insightful comment plus quotation/reference. 1 mark for more basic comment plus quotation/reference. 0 marks for quotation/reference alone. (Marks may be awarded 1+1.)	**2**	Possible answers include: ■ 'leftover hash' – the idea of making something from the remaining scraps (of the relationship) ■ 'soup … render from the bones' – the idea of squeezing the last possible scrap of nutrition, also the idea of totally destroying the relationship, of grinding it to dust ■ 'something substantial … tasty' – idea of being able to provide an ample meal (i.e. worthwhile topic of conversation about the relationship).
40			2 marks may be awarded for detailed/insightful comment plus quotation/reference. 1 mark for more basic comment plus quotation/reference. 0 marks for quotation/reference alone. (Marks may be awarded 2+2, 2+1+1 or 1+1+1+1.)	**4**	Possible answers include: ■ alliteration in 'cackling around the cauldron' suggests harsh, aggressive sound of their (witchlike) voices ■ onomatopoeic effect from 'spitting' – suggestion of contempt, disgust ■ alliteration/series of plosive consonants in 'spitting out the gristlier bits/of his giblets' suggests harshness, contempt, element of comedy also ■ echoic nature of 'bits of his giblets' – comic element, imitating their relish at the dismemberment ■ alliteration in 'gnawing on the knucklebone' – emphasised 'n' almost imitates gnawing sound ■ rhythmical similarity of 'intricate irony' echoes/mocks the faux-sophisticated conversation ■ alliteration in 'getting grave … -gout' suggests harsh, gritty nature of their voices.

Question			Expected response	Max. mark	Additional guidance
41			2 marks may be awarded for detailed/insightful comment plus quotation/reference. 1 mark for more basic comment plus quotation/reference. 0 marks for quotation/reference alone. (Marks may be awarded 2+2, 2+1+1 or 1+1+1+1.)	**4**	Possible answers include: ■ irony/double meaning in 'That's rich!' suggests self-consciously clever or unaware of what they're saying ■ word choice of 'splutter' suggests inelegant, lacking poise ■ imagery of 'munching the lies' suggests the enjoyment with which they accept/digest untruths about the man ■ simile of 'fat and sizzling as sausages' describes the 'lies' as unhealthy but appealing ■ word choice of 'sink back' suggests a smug self-satisfaction ■ metaphor 'gorged on truth' suggests bloated, self-satisfied; also ironic since they've been consuming lies ■ paradox in 'savage integrity' suggests their hypocrisy ■ word choice of 'sleek' suggests glossy, superficial, slightly smug ■ simile 'preening/like corbies' suggests they are predatory.
42			Candidates can answer in bullet points in this final question, or write a number of linked statements. Marks for this question should be allocated following the guidelines given at the start of these Marking Instructions. See page 132.	**10**	Possible references include: ■ *Last Supper* – the details in the extended metaphor about eating (e.g. 'leftover hash') are very tongue-in-cheek; the descriptions of 'The Girls' as witches ■ *For My Grandmother Knitting* – wordplay such as 'need/needles' and 'grasp of things'; the light-hearted reference to 'hands had forgotten/how to stop' ■ *My Rival's House* – wordplay such as 'her salt tears pepper our soup'; punning on 'surface' ■ *The Bargain* – wordplay such as 'fibreglass is flabbergasted' and 'buttonhopping stationpopping' ■ *Some Old Photographs* – the jokey, clichéd 'what-a-scorcher'; the idea of raindrops on a rainmate as 'sequins' ■ *View of Scotland/Love Poem* – the description of the mother's attachment to tradition is humorous (and affectionate): 'roller in with a waveset', 'giving it elbowgrease'.

Text 4 – Poetry – *Basking shark* by Norman MacCaig

Question			Expected response	Max. mark	Additional guidance
43			2 marks may be awarded for detailed/insightful comment plus quotation/reference. 1 mark for more basic comment plus quotation/reference. 0 marks for quotation/reference alone. (Marks may be awarded 2+2, 2+1+1 or 1+1+1+1.)	4	Possible answers include: ■ the rather convoluted sentence structure of lines 1–3 ('To ... To ... Is') suggests something unusual ■ 'where none should be' suggests something irrational, inexplicable ■ 'once (too often)' is paradoxical; and a distortion of the more usual, clichéd 'once too often' ■ the word 'slounge' is very unusual in itself (especially as a noun); it is onomatopoeic, suggesting a heavy, perhaps threatening movement ■ the vagueness of 'thing' adds to the weirdness of the event ■ the continued wordplay in 'But not too often, though enough' suggests a kind of baffled bemusement ■ 'a sea tin-tacked with rain' – a very descriptive metaphor, but also rather surreal ■ the contrast between the shark's physical size ('roomsized monster') and mental size ('matchbox brain') marks it out as peculiar.
44			2 marks may be awarded for detailed/insightful comment plus quotation/reference. 1 mark for more basic comment plus quotation/reference. 0 marks for quotation/reference alone. (Marks may be awarded 2+2, 2+1+1 or 1+1+1+1.)	4	Possible answers include: ■ the pun on 'displaced' (physical displacement of water by emerging from below the surface, and psychological effect on speaker) ■ 'shoggled' – use of a (rather unusual) Scots word gives it a homely conversational feel, minimises any idea of serious threat ■ referring to himself as a 'decadent townee' is self-mocking; the construction 'townee' suggests lack of importance ■ 'Shook on a wrong branch of his family tree' playfully mixes the usual idea of a family tree (as representing ancestry) with a literal tree (on a branch of which one might shake).

Question			Expected response	Max. mark	Additional guidance
45			2 marks may be awarded for detailed/insightful comment plus quotation/ reference. 1 mark for more basic comment plus quotation/ reference. 0 marks for quotation/ reference alone. (Marks may be awarded 1+1.)	2	Possible answers include: ■ because of a general belief that something unexpected ('Swish up the dirt ...') will lead to greater clarity ('... a spring/Is all the clearer') ■ the incident has caused him to reflect on evolution, his place in it and a sense of connection to his primordial origins ('the slime of everything') ■ hence his self-directed question: having instinctively classed the shark as a 'monster', he now wonders if he (as a representative of modern mankind) does not also have attributes of a 'monster'.
46			Candidates can answer in bullet points in this final question, or write a number of linked statements. Marks for this question should be allocated following the guidelines given at the start of these Marking Instructions. See page 132.	10	Possible references include: ■ *Basking shark* – the conclusion focuses on the slow exit of the shark, emphasised by a sequence of long vowels in 'sail', 'tall', 'slid away', 'tail'; leaves reader pondering the disturbing question 'who's the monster?', prompted by reflections on evolution ■ *Assisi* – the conclusion brings together the dwarf and St Francis, comparing the two in a playful, slightly ironic way ■ *Visiting hour* – the conclusion is bleak ('fruitless fruits ...') reflecting the speaker's emotional distress and feelings of inadequacy ■ *Sounds of the Day* – concludes with the startling 'hand-in-water' metaphor, which reinforces the way loss is felt first as a sudden sharpness, which then sinks in deeply ■ *Aunt Julia* – the conclusion reinforces the sense of loss, regret, of something not completed, which shows how the speaker feels about Aunt Julia ■ *Memorial* – concludes with complex imagery based on art ('elegy', 'masterpiece', 'fiction', 'music') to convey the power of her continuing presence, and the irony of his feelings being expressed in artistic terms.

Text 5 – Poetry – *I gave you immortality* by Sorley MacLean

Question			Expected response	Max. mark	Additional guidance
47			2 marks may be awarded for detailed/insightful comment plus quotation/reference. 1 mark for more basic comment plus quotation/reference. 0 marks for quotation/reference alone. (Marks may be awarded 2+2, 2+1+1 or 1+1+1+1.)	4	Possible answers include: ■ rather petulant tone of opening question 'I gave you … what did you …?' suggests he feels their relationship was one-sided ■ 'immortality' suggests his gift was of immense value, a timeless gift ■ 'only' implies he feels her gift was trivial by comparison ■ 'arrows' hints at the Cupid myth, but also suggests conflict and suffering ■ the imagery is extended in 'sharp … piercing … sore' suggesting she caused him extensive pain and misery ■ 'harsh' suggests the speaker feels he has suffered an injustice ■ 'sorrow' conveys emotional distress ■ 'bitterness' suggests the depth of his resentment ■ paradox ('sore gleam of glory') is a slightly poetic image (heightened by alliteration) but tempered by 'sore' ■ structure of 'If I gave … you gave it to me' suggests a turning of the tables, that she has unwittingly benefited him
					■ 'put an edge' suggests a sharpening, an improvement ■ 'radiance' suggests brilliance and enrichment ■ 'spoiled' suggests a negative effect, taking something away.
48			2 marks may be awarded for detailed/insightful comment plus quotation/reference. 1 mark for more basic comment plus quotation/reference. 0 marks for quotation/reference alone. (Marks may be awarded 1+1.)	2	Possible answers include: ■ use of subjunctives ('Were I …', 'I should …') suggests tentativeness, uncertainty ■ 'oblivion of my trouble' suggests that even if he could forget his anguish, the relief would be transitory ■ reference to 'Land of Youth' highlights his dreams of pleasure and delight before the realisation that his love would be unrequited ■ 'gracious' concedes how pleasing her beauty was and suggests his physical attraction to her was strong ■ 'although' introduces an admission of defeat ■ 'my weakness' suggests a realisation of his own frailty ■ 'again to be wounded' emphasises awareness of past suffering.

Question			Expected response	Max. mark	Additional guidance
49			2 marks may be awarded for detailed/insightful comment plus quotation/reference. 1 mark for more basic comment plus quotation/reference. 0 marks for quotation/reference alone. (Marks may be awarded 2+2, 2+1+1 or 1+1+1+1.)	4	Possible answers include: <ul><li>'O yellow-haired, lovely girl' – he still has powerful, emotional memories</li><li>'tore … inclined my course' – admits she had the power to move him, albeit diverting him from his 'aim'</li><li>'but' introduces an important rider: her distracting him has been an inspiration</li><li>'the fire of my lyric' suggests she has been a powerful influence/inspiration</li><li>'made a poet of me through sorrow' – his suffering at her hands has strengthened his creative powers</li><li>'pillar' suggests strength, monumental, supporting something of value</li><li>'memorial-stone' suggests religious intensity, something to last for ever</li><li>'till the Deluge' – Biblical reference to the end of time</li><li>idea in final two lines that his poetry (inspired by her) will be a lasting glory, while her beauty will fade.</li></ul>
50			Candidates can answer in bullet points in this final question, or write a number of linked statements. Marks for this question should be allocated following the guidelines given at the start of these Marking Instructions. See page 132.	10	Possible references include: <ul><li>*I gave you immortality* – intense imagery such as 'arrows', 'fire'; the willingness to conclude with 'the rotting of your beauty'</li><li>*Screapadal* – contempt/disgust at those who caused the Clearances, and for the forces behind the 'ships of death'</li><li>*An Autumn Day* – the terrifying description of the attack and the extended image of the six dead soldiers highlight his disgust at the futility of war</li><li>*Hallaig* – the references to the natural world (e.g. the personification of the trees) conveys his deep love for the natural landscape and/or his sadness at the effects of the Clearances</li><li>*Heroes* – his description of the 'poor little chap' as a very ordinary person conveys his disgust at the treatment of young soldiers in war</li><li>*Shores* – the importance of structure: three verses each set on a beach to convey the extent and scale of his love; the imagery of the ocean filling conveys his conviction that his love for her will last for eternity.</li></ul>

Text 6 – Poetry – *Two Trees* by Don Paterson

Question			Expected response	Max. mark	Additional guidance
51			2 marks may be awarded for detailed/insightful comment plus quotation/reference. 1 mark for more basic comment plus quotation/reference. 0 marks for quotation/reference alone. (Marks may be awarded 2+2, 2+1+1 or 1+1+1+1.)	4	Possible answers include: ■ standard, typical story opening 'One morning ...' ■ simplicity of '... got out of bed' ■ focuses on his 'one idea' and states it simply: 'to graft ...' ■ the hint that there is something potentially symbolic in what he is doing, i.e. attempting to bring together two different entities ■ keeps it focused on one person and his activities: 'work ... lay open ... lash' ■ 'twelve months' pass – the story moves on quickly ■ 'nothing' for a while, 'but one day ...', i.e. the next stage in the story has arrived ■ 'Over the years ...' – another long passage of time leading to ... ■ the wondrous outcome: 'each bough looked like it gave a double crop' ■ Miguel becomes a figure famous for his 'magic tree', i.e. he has (or appears to have) supernatural attributes.
52			2 marks may be awarded for detailed/insightful comment plus quotation/reference. 1 mark for more basic comment plus quotation/reference. 0 marks for quotation/reference alone. (Marks may be awarded 1+1.)	2	Possible answers include: ■ the new purchaser's lack of a 'dream' links back to Don Miguel's 'one idea' and forward to the potentially destructive nature of his action ■ his splitting of the tree links back to Don Miguel's successful grafting and forward to the effect of the separation ■ the 'fused seam' links back to Don Miguel's 'lash[ing]' them together and forward to the 'split[ting]' ■ 'two holes' links forward to the separation of the two trees and recalls Don Miguel's enthusiasm to turn two into one.

Question			Expected response	Max. mark	Additional guidance
53			2 marks may be awarded for detailed/insightful comment plus quotation/ reference. 1 mark for more basic comment plus quotation/ reference. 0 marks for quotation/ reference alone. (Marks may be awarded 2+2, 2+1+1 or 1+1+1+1.)	4	Possible answers include: ■ 'And no …' sounds almost as if addressed directly to readers who might be jumping ahead, warning them not to engage in fanciful interpretations ■ 'they did not … nor did … nor did' provides a list of the kind of interpretations readers might be expecting, and is forcefully negative about each one ■ the possible interpretations are all a little romanticised, whimsical (all involve anthropomorphism of a sort) almost in mockery of what readers might be expecting ■ concludes with two one-line sentences (the only ones in the poem) as if making a very simple, direct point ■ repetition of 'trees' emphasises that they are (he claims) the only topic of the poem ■ denies bluntly the possibility of trees having human qualities ('don't weep or ache or shout') ■ the assertiveness of the last two lines is emphasised by the straightforward, conclusive rhyme.
54			Candidates can answer in bullet points in this final question, or write a number of linked statements. Marks for this question should be allocated following the guidelines given at the start of these Marking Instructions. See page 132.	10	Possible references include: ■ *Two Trees* – symbolism in the grafting of the two trees, in their separation by the owner; in the (non-)consequences of their separation ■ *The Thread* – symbolism in idea of thread (as fragile but providing continuity), of the family as aeroplane rushing down the hill, the 'white dot' of the mother ■ *Waking With Russell* – symbolism in the 'true path' and 'mezzo del cammin' ideas; the smile as 'river' ■ *Nil Nil* – symbolism in the rise and fall of the football team's fortunes; in the pilot's crash; in the gallstone ■ *The Ferryman's Arms* – symbolism in the ferry/ ferryman; in the mysterious table ■ *11.00: Baldovan* – symbolism in the journey itself; in the bus stop as 'Steel flag'; in the coins.

Section 2 – Critical Essay – 20 marks

Supplementary marking grid

	Marks 20–19	Marks 18–16	Marks 15–13	Marks 12–10	Marks 9–6	Marks 5–0
Knowledge and understanding — The critical essay demonstrates:	thorough knowledge and understanding of the text	secure knowledge and understanding of the text	clear knowledge and understanding of the text	adequate knowledge and understanding of the text	limited evidence of knowledge and understanding of the text	very little knowledge and understanding of the text
	perceptive selection of textual evidence to support line of argument which is fluently structured and expressed	detailed textual evidence to support line of thought which is coherently structured and expressed	clear textual evidence to support line of thought which is clearly structured and expressed	adequate textual evidence to support line of thought which is adequately structured and expressed	limited textual evidence to support line of thought which is structured and expressed in a limited way	very little textual evidence to support line of thought which shows very little structure or clarity of expression
	perceptive focus on the demands of the question	secure focus on the demands of the question	clear focus on the demands of the question	adequate focus on the demands of the question	limited focus on the demands of the question	very little focus on the demands of the question
Analysis — The critical essay demonstrates:	perceptive analysis of the effect of features of language/filmic techniques	detailed analysis of the effect of features of language/filmic techniques	clear analysis of the effect of features of language/filmic techniques	adequate analysis of the effect of features of language/filmic techniques	limited analysis of the effect of features of language/filmic techniques	very little analysis of features of language/filmic techniques
Evaluation — The critical essay demonstrates:	committed evaluative stance with respect to the text and the task	engaged evaluative stance with respect to the text and the task	clear evaluative stance with respect to the text and the task	adequate evidence of an evaluative stance with respect to the text and the task	limited evidence of an evaluative stance with respect to the text and the task	very little evidence of an evaluative stance with respect to the text and the task
Technical Accuracy — The critical essay demonstrates:	few errors in spelling, grammar, sentence construction, punctuation and paragraphing the ability to be understood at first reading			adequate knowledge, sentence construction, punctuation	significant number of errors in spelling, grammar, sentence construction, punctuation and paragraphing which impedes understanding	

Practice Paper C

Paper 1: Reading for Understanding, Analysis and Evaluation

Passage 1

Question			Expected response	Max. mark	Additional guidance
1			Candidates must use their own words. No marks for straight lifts from the passage. 1 mark for each point from the 'Additional guidance' column.	4	Possible answers include: ■ the state had financial problems ■ the Governor devised a plan to alter the work pattern of most state employees ■ most state employees moved to a four-day week while working the same number of hours ■ the state saved a lot of money ■ there were benefits to the environment ■ the employees' health and work satisfaction improved ■ the employees quickly accepted and approved strongly of the scheme.
2			For full marks there should be comments on at least two examples. 2 marks may be awarded for detailed/insightful comment plus quotation/ reference. 1 mark for more basic comment plus quotation/ reference. 0 marks for quotation/ reference alone. (Marks may be awarded 2+2, 2+1+1 or 1+1+1+1.)	4	Possible answers include: ■ 'trapped' suggests imprisoned, confined ■ 'outdated' suggests old-fashioned, invalid ■ 'routine' suggests done without thinking, dull, boring ■ 'clung' suggests holding on desperately, reluctant to think of alternatives ■ 'religious devotion' suggests a possibly irrational belief in something with no foundation ■ 'Clock in, sit at your terminal, be seen to work, clock out' – listing of activities suggests a fixed, unshakeable pattern; minor sentence suggests that overall it is a dull, lifeless activity ■ rhetorical questions ('Is this ...', 'Should we ...') suggest the writer's contempt for the ideas in the questions ■ 'clamber' suggests unpleasant, ungainly movement involving discomfort ■ 'steel box ... concrete box' suggests car and office are both restrictive, inhuman.

Question			Expected response	Max. mark	Additional guidance
3			2 marks may be awarded for detailed/insightful comment plus quotation/reference. 1 mark for more basic comment plus quotation/reference. 0 marks for quotation/reference alone. (Marks may be awarded 2 or 1+1.)	2	Possible answers include: ■ parenthetical reference to *The Office* provides a specific example of the type of work the writer is referring to ■ repetition of 'constantly' reinforces the idea of an oppressive routine ■ list ('constantly … screen') suggests the large number of routine activities to be endured ■ repetition of 'better' emphasises the improvement in lifestyle that could be achieved ■ additional comment after the dash shows almost as an afterthought that there are even more benefits to be gained.
4	a)		Candidates must use their own words. No marks for straight lifts from the passage. For full marks, there must be reference to both the prediction and to the reality, but these do not have to be evenly divided. 2 marks may be awarded for detailed/insightful comment. 1 mark for more basic comment. 0 marks for quotation/reference alone. (Marks may be awarded 2+2, 2+1+1 or 1+1+1+1.)	4	Possible answers include: prediction: ■ once we reached the point when we had all we need as basics, work would feature less in our lives ■ the working week could be reduced to three days ■ we would be able to devote more time to leisure and culture reality: ■ rather than improving, the situation has become worse ■ despite people's wishes, we find ourselves working even longer hours ■ there is a culture of competitiveness and long hours which impacts on our health.
	b)		For full marks there should be comments on at least two examples. 2 marks may be awarded for detailed/insightful comment plus quotation/reference. 1 mark for more basic comment plus quotation/reference. 0 marks for quotation/reference alone. (Marks may be awarded 2+2, 2+1+1 or 1+1+1+1.)	4	Possible answers include: ■ 'scamper ever faster in our hamster-wheels' compares workers to caged animals engaged in repetitive, ultimately futile activity; suggests that we have no control, are simply doing as our bosses demand, have been drained of our humanity ■ 'treadmill is whirling ever-faster' compares working life to a gruelling, boring task of generating motion carried out by animals (or prisoners); suggests workers are mere functionaries, engaged in monotonous drudgery ■ 'locked in an arms race' compares workers to nations vying to outdo each other in the possession of ever more powerful weapons; suggests a pointless, dangerous escalation of competitiveness which no one can ever win.

Question			Expected response	Max. mark	Additional guidance
5			Candidates must use their own words. No marks for straight lifts from the passage. 2 marks may be awarded for detailed/insightful comment. 1 mark for more basic comment. (Marks may be awarded 2+1 or 1+1+1.)	3	Possible answers include: ■ there is more to life than constant work ■ serving the needs/demands of big business is not the most important thing in life ■ making money has a place in society, but it should not dominate us ■ precedence should be given to personal happiness ■ what matters is having sufficient time to appreciate life.
6			2 marks may be awarded for detailed/insightful comment plus quotation/reference. 1 mark for more basic comment plus quotation/reference. 0 marks for quotation/reference alone. (Marks may be awarded 2 or 1+1.)	2	Possible answers include: ■ the colon introduces an explanation of the metaphor 'arms treaty' ■ 'we all stop, together, now, at the 35 hour mark' is structured to sound like a list of crisp, military instructions ■ list of benefits ('became fitter … back to life') indicates the large number of benefits from the scheme ■ 'But' introduces the idea that there was a downside, that the benefits weren't allowed to last ■ the colon introduces an expansion of 'dismayed' and allows the paragraph to end on a simple statement of the people's feelings.
7			2 marks may be awarded for detailed/insightful comment plus quotation/reference. 1 mark for more basic comment plus quotation/reference. 0 marks for quotation/reference alone. (Marks may be awarded 2 or 1+1.)	2	Possible answers include: ■ 'a voice is calling' suggests an invocation of hope, a sort of mystical appeal ■ 'happier, healthier' suggests the improvement in mental and physical health to be gained ■ 'alternative' suggests there is another way, we do not have to accept the status quo ■ 'great free spaces beyond' suggests openness, liberation, unspoiled terrain.

Question on both passages

Question	Expected response	Max. mark	Additional guidance
8	Candidates may use bullet points in this final question, or write a number of linked statements. Evidence from the passage may include quotations, but these should be supported by explanations. The approach to marking is shown in the 'Additional guidance' column. Key areas of agreement are shown in the grid below. Other answers are possible.	5	The mark for this question should reflect the quality of response in two areas: ■ identification of the key areas of agreement in attitude/ideas ■ the level of detail given in support. The following guidelines should be used: ■ **5 marks** – identification of three key areas of agreement with insightful use of supporting evidence ■ **4 marks** – identification of three key areas of agreement with appropriate use of supporting evidence ■ **3 marks** – identification of three key areas of agreement ■ **2 marks** – identification of two key areas of agreement ■ **1 mark** – identification of one key area of agreement ■ **0 marks** – failure to identify one key area of agreement and/or misunderstanding of task. **NB** A candidate who identifies only two key areas of agreement may be awarded up to a maximum of 4 marks, as follows: ■ 2 marks for identification of two key areas of agreement **plus either** ■ a further 1 mark for appropriate use of supporting evidence to a total of 3 marks **or** ■ a further 2 marks for detailed/insightful use of supporting evidence to a total of 4 marks. A candidate who identifies only one key area of agreement may be awarded up to a maximum of 2 marks, as follows: ■ 1 mark for identification of one key area of agreement ■ a further 1 mark for use of supporting evidence to a total of 2 marks.

	Area of agreement	Passage 1	Passage 2
1	the role of work in our lives	we are locked into an outdated lifestyle dominated by work	work dominates the way we live; we work excessively long hours
2	there is more to life	leisure, culture, personal happiness should be encouraged	there are better, more fulfilling thigs to do (hobbies, family, culture, personal relationships)
3	effect on physical/mental health	increased incidence of stroke and heart attack	the prevalence of stress from overwork
4	past predictions about changes to work patterns	predictions of a three-day working week have proved wrong	predictions of a 15-hour working week have proved wrong
5	the power of big business	idea of 'serving corporations'; big business forced French government to withdraw the 35-hour maximum working week	our personal freedom is taken over by demands of 'bosses and employers'; we are 'in submission to them'
6	things are getting worse	the competitiveness which makes us need to seem to be working long hours	increase in pension age; more oppressive working patterns (zero-hours contracts, part-time work)
7	hope for the future	the schemes in Utah and in France demonstrate that change is possible and has many benefits	advances in technology should be exploited to reduce demands on humans' working lives

Paper 2: Critical Reading

Section 1 – Scottish Text – 20 marks

NB The final question (for 10 marks) on each text should be marked using the general instructions below. Text-specific guidance for each final question is given at the relevant point.

Up to 2 marks can be achieved for identifying elements of commonality as identified in the question.

A further 2 marks can be achieved for reference to the extract given.

6 additional marks can be achieved for discussion of similar references to at least one other part of the text (or to another short story or poem by the writer).

In practice this means:

- 2 marks for identification of **commonality**, e.g. theme, characterisation, use of imagery, setting, or any other key element.

From the **extract**:

- 2 marks for detailed/insightful comment plus quotation/reference
- 1 mark for more basic comment plus quotation/reference
- 0 marks for quotation/reference alone

From at least one **other part of the text** (or one other poem or short story):

- as above for up to 6 marks.

Text 1 – Drama – *The Slab Boys* by John Byrne

Question	Expected response	Max. mark	Additional guidance
1	2 marks may be awarded for detailed/insightful comment plus quotation/reference. 1 mark for more basic comment plus quotation/reference. 0 marks for quotation/reference alone. (Marks may be awarded 2+2, 2+1+1 or 1+1+1+1.)	4	Possible answers include: ■ the general idea that Hector is facing humiliation in his new clothing ■ the fact that the attempt by Alan to warn him is thwarted by Phil's threat with the pen such that (even) Alan is obliged to lie to him ■ Hector's pathetic enthusiasm: 'Will I go now and ask her? Will I?' ■ Phil and Spanky's apparent determination that he face humiliation at the hands not just of Lucille, but of Willie Curry also ■ Hector's enthusiasm for 'swanking' and his belief that his clothes are 'up to date' ■ the way he is forced into putting on the coat and the balaclava, showing him as at the mercy of others ■ Phil's justification for the balaclava ('it's draughty in Willie's room') verges on the insulting ■ the stage direction '*Slightly bamboozled*' paints him as a sad, put-upon figure ■ the glibness of Phil's invented story for him shows how much contempt he has for Hector, how much he enjoys manipulating him ■ the 'Triple pneumonia ... Double rupture ...' knockabout might amuse Phil and Spanky, but it is further evidence of their having fun at someone else's expense ■ Hector's 'I'll away along then' is pathetic in its simplicity and naivety ■ the insincerity of Phil and Spanky's good wishes ■ their bursting into uncontrollable laughter the moment he leaves.
2	2 marks may be awarded for detailed/insightful comment plus quotation/reference. 1 mark for more basic comment plus quotation/reference. 0 marks for quotation/reference alone. (Marks may be awarded 1+1.)	2	Possible answers include: ■ they make fun of Alan's rather public school turn of phrase 'a lousy trick' ■ they echo it sneeringly in similar terms: 'by jove' and 'you cad' ■ they mock Alan's (to them) posh way of speaking by pretending to speak in the same way.

Question			Expected response	Max. mark	Additional guidance
3			2 marks may be awarded for detailed/insightful comment plus quotation/ reference. 1 mark for more basic comment plus quotation/ reference. 0 marks for quotation/ reference alone. (Marks may be awarded 2+2, 2+1+1 or 1+1+1+1.)	4	Possible answers include: ■ the quite aggressive, forceful tone of 'Hey, watch it! Chuckit!' ■ Alan knows he's 'speaking out of turn', but is prepared this time to stand up to Phil ■ (for Alan) the use of 'poor little bastard' shows how angry he is, trying to make Phil see how awful things are going to be for Hector ■ he reels off what is going to happen to Hector ('thinking [...] he really does cut a dash ... he'll probably stop off ... doff the coat and hat') to paint a full scenario of Hector's humiliation as a result of Phil's behaviour ■ the rather extreme 'she'll wet herself' shows just how disastrous he thinks Phil's behaviour is ■ contempt in 'you and your crummy friend' ■ Phil's response is couched in mock public school language, implying that the ethics of the public school don't operate here ■ refers to Alan as 'Steerforth Minor', reducing Alan to a public school stereotype (with the added barb of 'Minor') ■ throws Alan's words 'poor little bastard' back at him, as if to say 'don't you dare call him that' ■ claims he and Spanky have some sort of right to humiliate Hector, as if there are situations Alan could never understand ■ Alan has the staying power to come back with 'More than a bit', showing he doesn't accept Phil's argument.
4			Candidates can answer in bullet points in this final question, or write a number of linked statements. Marks for this question should be allocated following the guidelines given at the start of these Marking Instructions. See page 165.	10	Possible references include: ■ Alan is the butt of many of Phil's jokes and sarcasm, providing much of the humour of the play and helping to characterise Phil as a spokesman for rebellious youth ■ Alan represents the successful, privileged middle class that Phil despises, is part of the class system which the play explores through Phil's sense of alienation and unfair treatment ■ Alan is the antithesis of Phil in terms of work ethic, conventional manners, respect for 'superiors', often causing the audience to question the validity, sincerity of Phil's extreme opinions.

Text 2 – Drama – *The Cheviot, the Stag and the Black, Black Oil* by John McGrath

Question			Expected response	Max. mark	Additional guidance
5			2 marks may be awarded for detailed/insightful comment plus quotation/reference. 1 mark for more basic comment plus quotation/reference. 0 marks for quotation/reference alone. (Marks may be awarded 1+1.)	2	Possible answers include: ■ the idea that 'The landlords had an ally in the heart of the community' prepares the audience to expect someone who is two-faced, duplicitous, treacherous; when it is revealed to be the Minister, disapproval of the Church is obvious ■ having the fiddle play the psalm tune is mockingly ironic, providing a mock-respectful musical backdrop for the Minister ■ similarly, the company humming the tune quietly during the donning of the costume is ironically mocking the solemnity of the occasion ■ dressing one of the actors as a minister might be seen as mocking in itself, as if anyone can take on the role, it is nothing special.

6			2 marks may be awarded for detailed/insightful comment plus quotation/reference.
			1 mark for more basic comment plus quotation/reference.
			0 marks for quotation/reference alone.
			(Marks may be awarded 2+2, 2+1+1 or 1+1+1+1.)
				4	Possible answers include:
					■ 'Dearly beloved Brethren' is a standard opening invocation
					■ repetition of 'Lord' (satirically overdone in opening sentence)
					■ use of capitals ('Lord ... His ... He') to suggest reverence in the voice
					■ rhetorical devices such as:
					  ■ use of direct address ('Oh guilty sinners')
					  ■ repetition ('How many times and on how many Sabbaths')
					  ■ use of figurative/metaphorical language – some is pretty standard ('Shepherd ... paths of righteousness', 'troubles ... visiting'), some is rather fanciful ('tents of iniquity')
					  ■ periodic sentence ('On that fearful day ...')
					■ quotation from Scripture: 'I will repay'
					■ old-fashioned diction: 'the wrath of the Almighty', 'saith', 'everybody here gathered'
					■ frequently admonitory tone – 'your wickedness', 'so far neglected the dignity of your womanhood', 'answer for their flagrant transgression of authority'.

Question			Expected response	Max. mark	Additional guidance
7			2 marks may be awarded for detailed/insightful comment plus quotation/ reference. 1 mark for more basic comment plus quotation/ reference. 0 marks for quotation/ reference alone. For full marks both this section and what has preceded should be covered but not necessarily in equal measure. (Marks may be awarded 2+2, 2+1+1 or 1+1+1+1.)	**4**	Possible answers include: what has preceded: ■ is static (just one person speaking) ■ is tedious in tone (though designed to be humorous as a result) ■ is threatening in tone ■ is dominated by male authority figure ■ is critical of women this section: ■ is lively and animated, with entrances, cheers, groans, leaping on stage, dancing … ■ is celebratory: Girl reels off names of the rebel townships ■ is dominated by females rejecting, dismissing, challenging authority ■ employs uplifting, 'call-to-arms' language: 'stout resistance', 'burning the summonses', 'second line of defence' ■ praises women's fortitude and non-violence.
8			Candidates can answer in bullet points in this final question, or write a number of linked statements. Marks for this question should be allocated following the guidelines given at the start of these Marking Instructions. See page 165.	**10**	Possible references include: ■ Andy McChuckemup: patter of the Glasgow wide-boy ('picture it, if yous will') ■ Texas Jim: stereotype of rapacious American businessman; glib rhyming couplets in square dance ('8 9 10 11 12/Billions of dollars all to myself') ■ Lord Polwarth: bureaucratic gobbledegook ('A broad forum to cover the whole spectrum') ■ Duke of Sutherland: ornate, pompous, clichéd xenophobia ('cruel despotic Tsar', 'Mongol hordes') ■ Sellar: panegyric to Duke of Sutherland delivered in ridiculously high-flown language ■ Minister: overblown 'biblical' language used to threaten not console ■ Lady Phosphate/Lord Crask: mock-upper-class ('– what', 'Topping' etc.) ■ Lord Vat: professes romantic view of Highlanders ('they have proved excellent servants') – but is easily bought.

Text 3 – Drama – *Men Should Weep* by Ena Lamont Stewart

Question	Expected response	Max. mark	Additional guidance
9	2 marks may be awarded for detailed/insightful comment plus quotation/reference. 1 mark for more basic comment plus quotation/reference. 0 marks for quotation/reference alone. (Marks may be awarded 2+1 or 1+1+1.)	3	Possible answers include: ■ her appearance (make-up, clothing, hair) suggests someone rather brazen, shameless, unconcerned with appearances ■ 'Leave me go' suggests defiance, aggression, no fear of father ■ *'shakes herself free'* suggests independence, lack of respect for father ■ *'glaring at each other'* suggests she is strong-willed, not intimidated by her father ■ '... in front o ma friend' suggests concern for status, lack of concern for father's point of view, perhaps taunting him with unknown 'friend' ■ 'nane o your business', 'Nane o your damned interferin business' suggests prepared to insult, defy her father, use provocative language ■ 'I'm grown up noo' suggests she is assertive, tired of being treated like a child ■ 'An I tellt ye!' suggests anger in her voice, standing up for herself.
10	2 marks may be awarded for detailed/insightful comment plus quotation/reference. 1 mark for more basic comment plus quotation/reference. 0 marks for quotation/reference alone. (Marks may be awarded 2+2, 2+1+1 or 1+1+1+1.)	4	Possible answers include: ■ the fact that all the speeches in these lines are short and aggressive, frequently indicated by use of exclamation marks ■ John grabs her – physical hostility ■ the aggression in 'Where wis ye? Answer me!' – harsh question and command ■ Jenny's sullen, minimal response 'At the pickshers' ■ John's relentless demand for more information (to begin with he wanted to know where she was, now it's where she was after that) ■ her behaviour when he lets her go – *'flops'* suggesting lack of respect; *'glaring sullenly'* showing her antagonism; *'rubbing her shoulder'* to remind John (and the audience) of his manhandling of her ■ John, with both questions answered, presses on with dismissive comment about her friend – 'yon' sounds contemptuous ■ Jenny's provocative response 'That's a peety. I dae.'

Question			Expected response	Max. mark	Additional guidance
					■ John resorts to insulting language: 'Ye impident little bitch!' ■ the open threat of more violence: 'tak ma belt tae ye' ■ Jenny's dismissive, sneering, challenging, defiant 'Jist you try it!'
11			2 marks may be awarded for detailed/insightful comment plus quotation/reference. 1 mark for more basic comment plus quotation/reference. 0 marks for quotation/reference alone. (Marks may be awarded 2+1 or 1+1+1.)	3	Possible answers include: ■ 'paint smeared' – he belittles her appearance, 'paint' instead of 'make-up' suggesting garish, unsophisticated; 'smeared' suggesting something messy, unattractive ■ 'a ower yer face' – as if she has applied it randomly, made herself look hideous ■ 'Look at yersel!' – antagonistic exclamation, implying she looks a mess ■ *drags ... propels ... holding ... scrubs* – violent, aggressive actions suggesting his temper ■ 'There!' – a sort of triumphant declaration of his victory ■ 'the colour God meant it tae be' – self-righteous, pompous moralising.
12			Candidates can answer in bullet points in this final question, or write a number of linked statements. Marks for this question should be allocated following the guidelines given at the start of these Marking Instructions. See page 165.	10	Possible references include: ■ she is characterised as a rebel, an independent spirit, not prepared to put up with poverty and degradation ■ she is structurally important: her three appearances (arriving home late; leaving; returning with offer of money) are key moments in the play and in the development of John and Maggie's relationship ■ she is prepared at an early stage to challenge her parents' authority ■ her assertion of independence by giving up her job and then by leaving home is an important strand in the theme of the changing roles of men and women at the time ■ she is the one who points out most forcefully the squalor in which they live ■ her successful challenge to her father's refusal to accept tainted money at the end of the play is an important catalyst for Maggie's change of viewpoint ■ the mixed emotions she brings out in John serve to show what a confused, weak character he is ■ her capacity for kindness and decency at the end are part of the healing process in the family.

Text 1 – Prose – *The Painter* by Iain Crichton Smith

Question			Expected response	Max. mark	Additional guidance
13			2 marks may be awarded for detailed/insightful comment plus quotation/reference. 1 mark for more basic comment plus quotation/reference. 0 marks for quotation/reference alone. For full marks both sides of the ambiguity should be covered but not necessarily in equal measure. (Marks may be awarded 2+2, 2+1+1 or 1+1+1+1.)	4	Possible answers include: suggestions that it is serious: ■ the ferocity suggested by word choice of 'kill … enraged … frustrated … tortured' ■ the metaphor in 'gradually grew more demoniac' suggests father-in-law is almost possessed ■ details of actual injury in 'cutting his son-in-law's left leg so that he fell to the ground' suggests severity of the attack suggestions that it may not be serious: ■ inclusion of 'perhaps', 'to a certain extent' suggest narrator's uncertainty ■ 'however' (used twice) shows a willingness to contradict himself, lessen the seriousness of what has just been said ■ 'ponderously' suggests rather lethargic movement ■ 'looked … as if …' suggests speculation, lack of certainty ■ 'odd … as if each was trying to cut corn' – they're merely 'odd', not frightening, and appear as if engaged on everyday activity ■ description of wife is essentially comic.
14			2 marks may be awarded for detailed/insightful comment plus quotation/reference. 1 mark for more basic comment plus quotation/reference. 0 marks for quotation/reference alone. For full marks both William and the fighters should be covered but not necessarily in equal measure. (Marks may be awarded 2+2, 2+1+1 or 1+1+1+1.)	4	Possible answers include: William: ■ 'sitting comfortably' suggests he is relaxed ■ 'no expression on his face at all' suggests he is emotionless ■ 'a cold clear intensity' suggests a deep, almost disturbing concentration ■ 'as if he were asleep' suggests he is detached ■ 'he sat there' suggests he is passive ■ 'nor … did he make any attempt to pull his chair back' suggests he is unaware of (or not bothered by) any danger the fighters: ■ 'the scythes swung to and fro' suggests repeated intense and dangerous activity ■ 'faces … contorted' suggests the effort is twisting the shape of their faces ■ 'in the fury of battle' suggests a sense of ferocious engagement ■ 'suffused with blood and rage' suggests a sense of all-consuming anger ■ 'teeth were drawn back in a snarl' suggests an animal-like savagery.

Question			Expected response	Max. mark	Additional guidance
15			2 marks may be awarded for detailed/insightful comment plus quotation/reference. 1 mark for more basic comment plus quotation/reference. 0 marks for quotation/reference alone. (Marks may be awarded 1+1.)	2	Possible answers include: ■ revulsion at his coldness, callousness ■ thinks he is as unfeeling as a natural predator ■ compares his response with a rat, i.e. aggressive when challenged ■ resents his apparent assumption that events had been organised for his benefit ■ his attitude reduces human participants to inanimate objects ('house ... wall') ■ [possibly] recognises in William the urge to capture that he, as a writer, shares.
16			Candidates can answer in bullet points in this final question, or write a number of linked statements. Marks for this question should be allocated following the guidelines given at the start of these Marking Instructions. See page 165.	10	Possible references include: ■ *The Painter* – the narrator's sudden rage against William; William's unexpected disappearance from the village ■ *The Telegram* – the elder's passing by both houses; the revelation of the true contents of the telegram ■ *In Church* – the finding of a church so close to the front line; encountering the occupant of the church; the nature of the 'minister's' sermon; the shock ending ■ *The Crater* – the events when they reach the German trench; the shock of the soldier's death after all the effort to rescue him ■ *The Red Door* – the discovery of the red door; Murdo's resolve to visit Mary ■ *Mother and Son* – the build-up to the point when it seems John will be violent; the unexpected passivity of the conclusion.

Text 2 – Prose – *The Eye of the Hurricane* by George Mackay Brown

Question			Expected response	Max. mark	Additional guidance
17			2 marks may be awarded for detailed/insightful comment plus quotation/reference. 1 mark for more basic comment plus quotation/reference. 0 marks for quotation/reference alone. (Marks may be awarded 2+2, 2+1+1 or 1+1+1+1.)	4	Possible answers include: ■ very matter-of-fact opening ('Now, Barclay, about this cold of mine') as if the whole conversation will be businesslike, not admitting of any disagreement ■ disparages Miriam early on, an attempt to neutralise her influence on the narrator, to get him 'on-side' ■ tells narrator that his drinking is not something he can control, claims it's a natural phenomenon which has to be faced up to ■ addresses him like teacher/pupil: 'Do you understand that, Barclay?' ■ flatters the narrator with a reference to his writing ■ ingratiates himself with the narrator ('I like you. I'm very glad you're living in this house.') ■ uses an elaborate seagoing metaphor to justify asking narrator to help ■ asserts his dominant role as 'skipper' ■ tries to make it simple: 'And the first thing I want you to do ...' ■ completely ignores the narrator's repeated refusals ■ resorts to open threat of raising rent, evicting him.
18			2 marks may be awarded for detailed/insightful comment plus quotation/reference. 1 mark for more basic comment plus quotation/reference. 0 marks for quotation/reference alone. (Marks may be awarded 2+2, 2+1+1 or 1+1+1+1.)	4	Possible answers include: ■ 'Charity is no hard-minted currency ... a shilling here and a sovereign there': it is not a simple matter of tangible coinage, cash to be handed out as and when you wish ■ 'it is the oil and wine that drop uncertainly through the fingers': it is like liquid, not easily defined, not easily controlled ■ 'the wounds of the world': the idea that suffering can happen at any time in any place ■ 'wherever the roads of pity and suffering cross': compares pain and the compassion to alleviate it to roads which, when they intersect, allow 'charity' to be delivered.
19			2 marks may be awarded for detailed/insightful comment plus quotation/reference. 1 mark for more basic comment plus quotation/reference. 0 marks for quotation/reference alone. (Marks may be awarded 1+1.)	2	Possible answers include: ■ pity – sees him as a lonely, lost figure, caught up in his own fantasies ■ concern – the constant pacing must be indicative of mental struggle.

Question			Expected response	Max. mark	Additional guidance
20			Candidates can answer in bullet points in this final question, or write a number of linked statements. Marks for this question should be allocated following the guidelines given at the start of these Marking Instructions. See page 165.	10	Possible references include: ■ *The Eye of the Hurricane* – Barclay confronts Captain Stevens on several occasions; also confronts Jansen and Hackland ■ *Tartan* – the Vikings have confrontations with the community as a whole, with Malcolm, with Duncan's son ■ *A Time To Keep* – Bill has confrontations with the factor, Ingi's father, the men from Two Waters ■ *The Whaler's Return* – Flaws has confrontations with Small, the minister, the tinkers ■ *The Wireless Set* – Betsy 'confronts' Lord Haw-Haw ■ *The Bright Spade* – idea of confrontation between the community and the elements.

Text 3 – Prose – *The Trick Is To Keep Breathing* by Janice Galloway

Question			Expected response	Max. mark	Additional guidance
21			2 marks may be awarded for detailed/insightful comment plus quotation/reference. 1 mark for more basic comment plus quotation/reference. 0 marks for quotation/reference alone. (Marks may be awarded 2+2, 2+1+1 or 1+1+1+1.)	4	Possible answers include: ■ his arrival is announced by 'gravel and the crunch of brakes', suggesting something noisy, grating, impatient; he is de-personalised ■ 'stare harder' suggests that the thought of his arrival causes her to tense up ■ his approach is described menacingly in terms of feet getting closer ■ 'thudding' is a harsh, pounding sound, intimidating ■ his flaunting of the bottle suggests someone rather brash, showy ■ the 'clumsy orchid' description associates him with a distortion of beauty ■ 'Always take it for granted I'm going to win' reeks of (over-)confidence (and possible double entendre) ■ the 'lips ... beard ... teeth' references suggest something vaguely animal-like, rather unsettling ■ the clichéd compliments ('a real picture') are repeated *ad nauseam*.

Question			Expected response	Max. mark	Additional guidance
22			2 marks may be awarded for detailed/insightful comment plus quotation/reference. 1 mark for more basic comment plus quotation/reference. 0 marks for quotation/reference alone. (Marks may be awarded 1+1.)	2	Possible answers include: <ul><li>the fact that it is an entirely one-sided conversation; Joy says nothing</li><li>'It plays Country and Western Music' – surreal idea of car as animate object</li><li>'The seat creaks with his weight' suggests he is overweight, oppressive</li><li>Tony's remarks are laden with innuendo, cheap come-ons ('Nearly as good as you', 'Expect a treat tonight')</li><li>'He pats my leg' suggests making unwelcome advances</li><li>his overtly suggestive pausing at *'it's hard ...'* waiting for a response</li><li>his leering way of looking at her, which is repeated after every sentence.</li></ul>
23			2 marks may be awarded for detailed/insightful comment plus quotation/reference. 1 mark for more basic comment plus quotation/reference. 0 marks for quotation/reference alone. (Marks may be awarded 2+2, 2+1+1 or 1+1+1+1.)	4	Possible answers include: <ul><li>short, clipped sentences suggest not much of a conversationalist, sees everything in simple terms</li><li>all one-way – suggests he's not interested in what Joy might have to say, single-mindedly pursuing his simple goal of seducing her</li><li>references to her weight, to her illness suggest high level of insensitivity</li><li>references to her appearance and potential for being a 'stunner' reveal him as sexist, old-fashioned</li><li>'Just relax and listen to the music' sounds deeply insincere</li><li>'This one's my favourite' suggests he can't avoid self-centredness</li><li>'You don't mind if I run it again' is a statement rather than a question: he's going to do it regardless of any opinion Joy might have</li><li>'Hiding your best assets' – a lewd comment</li><li>perhaps genuine shock, concern when he asks about her hands.</li></ul>

Question	Expected response	Max. mark	Additional guidance
24	Candidates can answer in bullet points in this final question, or write a number of linked statements. Marks for this question should be allocated following the guidelines given at the start of these Marking Instructions. See page 165.	10	Possible references include: ■ Paul: teenage/school romance; fails largely because Joy defines her relationship with him in terms of domesticity, but his primary concern is sex ■ David: potentially inappropriate relationship with ex-pupil; there is some genuine feeling between them, but both realise it cannot be a lasting relationship; their drunken sex on his Sunday visits (and her elaborate preparations for these) suggest her need for companionship and his willingness to exploit her ■ Michael: secret affair with married colleague; when his wife finds out, he and Joy plan life together; his death on holiday prevents this and its effect on Joy dominates the whole text ■ Tony: the oppressive boss, whose flirtations Joy tolerates up to a point; he takes advantage of her with no concern for her vulnerability; she knows the kind of person he is, but seems unable to reject him wholly ■ other men (e.g. doctors at hospital): generally passive; her internal musings show she can see through them, but she rarely expresses her feelings about them openly.

Text 4 – Prose – *Sunset Song* by Lewis Grassic Gibbon

Question	Expected response	Max. mark	Additional guidance
25	2 marks may be awarded for detailed/insightful comment plus quotation/reference. 1 mark for more basic comment plus quotation/reference. 0 marks for quotation/reference alone. (Marks may be awarded 2+2, 2+1+1 or 1+1+1+1.)	4	Possible answers include: ■ 'shame'/'shamed' suggests that non-users of Scots/Scotch are a source of dishonour, humiliation ■ 'the split-tongued sourocks' suggests a contemptuous attitude, accusation of hypocrisy ■ 'Every damned little narrow dowped rat' is all-inclusive condemnation of English-speakers ('Every'); contemptible ('damned'); insubstantial, lacking substance ('little', 'narrow dowped'); loathsome, to be looked down on ('rat') ■ 'put on (the English)' suggests the use of English is forced, affected, pretentious ■ 'thin bit scraichs' suggests he thinks of English as weak, anaemic, shrill, strident ■ *You can tell me, man ...*' Rob's tone is quite belligerent, challenging Gordon to dare to disagree.

Question	Expected response	Max. mark	Additional guidance
26	2 marks may be awarded for detailed/insightful comment plus quotation/reference. 1 mark for more basic comment plus quotation/reference. 0 marks for quotation/reference alone. (Marks may be awarded 1+1.)	2	Possible answers include: ■ repetition ('coarse, coarse', 'work, work, work, and chave, chave, chave') stresses the amount of effort required, echoes the repetitive nature of the work ■ 'from the blink of day till the fall of night' conveys the extreme length of the working day ■ 'soss and sotter' – the alliteration/onomatopoeia emphasises the filth, unpleasantness of the work.
27	2 marks may be awarded for detailed/insightful comment plus quotation/reference. 1 mark for more basic comment plus quotation/reference. 0 marks for quotation/reference alone. (Marks may be awarded 2+2, 2+1+1 or 1+1+1+1.)	4	Possible answers include: ■ there are four different (reported) speakers involved: Cuddiestoun, banker's son, Chae, Long Rob; shows range of views being put forward ■ sentence openers ('Syne ... So ... But ... And') indicate different points of view being proposed ■ 'childe' suggests contempt for banker's son, suggests naïve, inexperienced ■ 'clutter of machines' presents machinery as untidy, chaotic, not effective ■ *the best friend of man* suggests human quality, of extreme usefulness ■ Chae's forceful tone: *'Damn't, no ...'* ■ Rob's mocking, humorous tone: 'damned machine that would muck you a pigsty even though they all turned socialist to-morrow'.
28	Candidates can answer in bullet points in this final question, or write a number of linked statements. Marks for this question should be allocated following the guidelines given at the start of these Marking Instructions. See page 165.	10	Possible references include: ■ the closeness of the community, providing mutual support (e.g. the fire at Peesie's Knapp, the funeral, the wedding, the dedication of the war memorial) ■ the centrality of the land and the seasons ■ Chris's decision to stay on the farm; her attachment to the land ■ the importance of the Standing Stones as symbols of permanence ■ the impact of the War – on individuals (e.g. Ewan) and on the land (e.g. the stripping away of the forests) ■ developments in farming – technological (e.g. the new binders) and ownership (e.g. the amalgamation of the smaller farms after the War) ■ changes in the role of women (e.g. acknowledgement of sexuality – Mollie Douglas; taking control of their lives – Marget Strachan).

Text 5 – Prose – *The Cone-Gatherers* by Robin Jenkins

Question			Expected response	Max. mark	Additional guidance
29			2 marks may be awarded for detailed/insightful comment plus quotation/reference. 1 mark for more basic comment plus quotation/reference. 0 marks for quotation/reference alone. (Marks may be awarded 1+1.)	2	Possible answers include: ▪ the balancing around the semicolon helps to convey the idea that Calum has changed from being a beater to thinking of himself as a deer ▪ the sentence beginning 'He could not, however …' serves to introduce the contrast between the deer's agility and Calum's clumsiness ▪ the structure of the sentence beginning 'He fell and rose again …' imitates the frantic, headlong action it describes with a list of movements ('fell … rose … avoided … collide'); it also lists all the things Calum feels are ignoring him and the deer, so many that he feels completely cut off from help or sympathy.
30			2 marks may be awarded for detailed/insightful comment plus quotation/reference. 1 mark for more basic comment plus quotation/reference. 0 marks for quotation/reference alone. (Marks may be awarded 2+2, 2+1+1 or 1+1+1+1.)	4	Possible answers include: ▪ 'barked fiercely' suggests harsh, loud, aggressive noise ▪ 'rush into the danger' suggests a reckless dash ▪ 'roared to him' suggests an impassioned, panicked cry ▪ 'resounded with their exultant shouts' suggests an echoing effect, all the calls mixing together ▪ 'bellowed' suggests loud, deep, fanatical ▪ 'bawled' suggests frantic, hysterical ▪ the list of adjectives, 'silent, desperate, and heroic', suggests the extent of their plight ▪ 'guns banged' suggests loud, aggressive noise, associated with death/violence ▪ 'wails of lament' suggests high-pitched exclamations of mourning ▪ 'dashed on at demented speed' suggests reckless speed, desperate, almost out of control ▪ 'shot out' suggests a sudden, dramatic appearance ▪ 'a deer screaming' suggests high-pitched, suffering, in pain ▪ 'scrabbling about' suggests agitated, distressed movement ▪ 'feverishly reloading' suggests excited, tense movement ▪ the rather paradoxical 'Screaming in sympathy' suggests the confusion at the scene ▪ the list of actions 'flung … clasped … tried to comfort' suggests a rush of actions ▪ 'flung' suggests acting with passion, no thought of consequences ▪ 'dragged him about with it in its mortal agony' suggests frantic movement back and forth at the moment of death.

Question			Expected response	Max. mark	Additional guidance
31			2 marks may be awarded for detailed/insightful comment plus quotation/ reference. 1 mark for more basic comment plus quotation/ reference. 0 marks for quotation/ reference alone. (Marks may be awarded 2+2, 2+1+1 or 1+1+1+1.)	4	Possible answers include: ■ the contrast between the immobility of Forgan, Roderick and Lady Runcie-Campbell, and Duror 'leaping out of the wood' like something possessed, emphasises Duror's disturbed state of mind ■ the paradoxical 'berserk joy' depicts him as out of control, unaware of what his real emotions are ■ the blunt abruptness of the simple sentence 'There was a knife in his hand' focuses attention on it and foreshadows the violent act he is about to carry out ■ 'he never heard' suggests he is switched off, so caught up in his emotions that he cannot process the sound of her words ■ 'Rushing ... he threw ... with furious force, ... seizing ... cut its throat savagely' combine to depict someone in an uncontrolled, violent bloodlust, acting with tremendous strength and energy ■ the ambiguity of his pose after the kill, not proud, but apparently grieving, suggests a confusion in his own mind ■ clinging onto the knife suggests he is in shock, doesn't know what to do.
32			Candidates can answer in bullet points in this final question, or write a number of linked statements. Marks for this question should be allocated following the guidelines given at the start of these Marking Instructions. See page 165.	10	Possible references include: ■ Calum as the personification of innocence ■ the disconnect between his physical appearance and his inner beauty ■ his identification/empathy with nature (the rabbit, the chaffinches) ■ his agility in the trees and love of the freedom, solitude there ■ his trust in Neil ■ his lack of malice towards the upper classes (in contrast to Neil) ■ his discomfort in company (the pub) ■ his behaviour at the deer drive ■ his childlike desires (the doll) ■ his inability to comprehend Duror's malice ■ his Christ-like death.

Text 1 – Poetry – *Tam o' Shanter* by Robert Burns

Question	Expected response	Max. mark	Additional guidance
33	2 marks may be awarded for detailed/insightful comment plus quotation/reference. 1 mark for more basic comment plus quotation/reference. 0 marks for quotation/reference alone. (Marks may be awarded 2+2, 2+1+1 or 1+1+1+1.)	4	Possible answers include: ■ 'As bees …' suggests a sense of outrage, a need to escape assault; idea of the small and vulnerable ('bees') being threatened by something larger ('herds') ■ 'As open pussie's …' suggests a sudden ('pop') attack close at hand ('before their nose') which causes extreme alarm ■ 'As eager …' suggests a concerted response to a rallying cry, one being chased by many.
34	2 marks may be awarded for detailed/insightful comment plus quotation/reference. 1 mark for more basic comment plus quotation/reference. 0 marks for quotation/reference alone. (Marks may be awarded 2+2, 2+1+1 or 1+1+1+1.)	4	Possible answers include: ■ the pause to lecture Tam creates tension by delaying the continuation of the story ■ the direct address to Meg ('do thy speedy utmost') reminds reader of the urgency involved ■ setting a sort of target for Meg/Tam ('There at them …') sets up the dramatic chase, creating uncertainty about their fate ■ idea of Nannie being way out in front of the other witches creates fear that she will catch Tam ■ referring to Maggie as 'noble' increases the sense of good versus evil in the chase ■ the frantic efforts by Nannie ('flew at Tam wi' furious ettle') increase the tension ■ 'But little wist she …' – a last-minute turn of fortune, the hero has a trick up his sleeve ■ 'Ae spring' – a single leap, one last final effort ■ 'But left behind …' – the sacrifice involved in saving her master.

Question			Expected response	Max. mark	Additional guidance
35			2 marks may be awarded for detailed/insightful comment plus quotation/reference. 1 mark for more basic comment plus quotation/reference. 0 marks for quotation/reference alone. (Marks may be awarded 2+2, 2+1+1 or 1+1+1+1.)	2	Possible answers include: ■ not serious: it's just a conventional conclusion, with the expected element of moralising and instruction ('take heed … Think … Remember'); it can't really be a 'tale o' truth' so any resultant moral isn't convincing; it's just a bit of fun, developing the idea of men as in need of guidance, playing on superstitions of witchcraft; the way that 'tale' puns on 'tail' (line 24) can be seen as making light of the whole idea ■ serious: it warns reasonably enough about over-indulgence (in drink or lascivious thoughts), of paying a high price for unwise behaviour; it is addressed only to men, the weaker sex as far as irresponsible behaviour is concerned.
36			Candidates can answer in bullet points in this final question, or write a number of linked statements. Marks for this question should be allocated following the guidelines given at the start of these Marking Instructions. See page 165.	10	Possible references include: ■ *Tam o' Shanter* – passes judgement on men in general (and Tam in particular) for their drunkenness, their foolhardy behaviour when drunk, their easy attraction to a pretty woman ■ *To a Mouse* – passes judgement on mankind in general for its careless attitude to nature and for its self-absorption ■ *Holy Willie's Prayer* – passes judgement on Hamilton, on Holy Willie himself, on the Kirk in general ■ *A Man's a Man for a' That* – passes judgement on the nobility, the upper classes and on the pompous in general; also by implication on those who respect wealth and status ■ *A Poet's Welcome to his Love-Begotten Daughter* – passes judgement on the Kirk, on all who criticise him for fathering a child out of wedlock and on those who think he is not a loving father ■ *Address to the Deil* – passes judgement (by implication) on those who believe in the traditional concept of the devil and perhaps on those who look down on old country ways.

Text 2 – Poetry – *Valentine* by Carol Ann Duffy

Question			Expected response	Max. mark	Additional guidance
37			2 marks may be awarded for detailed/insightful comment plus quotation/reference. 1 mark for more basic comment plus quotation/reference. 0 marks for quotation/reference alone. (Marks may be awarded 2+2, 2+1+1 or 1+1+1+1.)	4	Possible answers include: ■ starting with a negative 'Not a …' ■ the abruptness of the minor sentence, which constitutes not just a line on its own but a stanza/verse paragraph ■ the feeling that it is part of an ongoing conversation ■ the bizarre idea of 'an onion' as a substitute for the conventional 'red rose' or 'satin heart' ■ the use of present tense makes it immediate, direct ■ series of short sentences sounds staccato, breathless ■ 'moon wrapped in brown paper' suggests a startling contradiction ■ comparison of 'light' to 'the careful undressing of love' is hard to fathom.
38			2 marks may be awarded for detailed/insightful comment plus quotation/reference. 1 mark for more basic comment plus quotation/reference. 0 marks for quotation/reference alone. (Marks may be awarded 2+2, 2+1+1 or 1+1+1+1.)	4	Possible answers include: ■ 'blind you with tears' suggests the power of love to cause unhappiness ■ 'a wobbling photo of grief' suggests the distorted view a victim of love may have ■ repetition of 'It will …' suggests a relentlessness in love's power to hurt ■ 'I am trying to be truthful' sounds like an assertion to an unheard listener who is trying to reject the speaker's claims ■ the alliteration in 'a cute card or a kissogram' seems to be suggesting/mocking the childishness of the traditional message ■ 'fierce kiss' suggests the lingering aftertaste of the onion – the difficulty of escaping a relationship ■ 'possessive' suggests jealousy/the desire to control ■ juxtaposition of 'possessive' and 'faithful' undermines the normally positive view of commitment.

Question			Expected response	Max. mark	Additional guidance
39			2 marks may be awarded for detailed/insightful comment plus quotation/reference. 1 mark for more basic comment plus quotation/reference. 0 marks for quotation/reference alone. (Marks may be awarded 1+1.)	2	Possible answers include: ■ the imperative 'Take it' suggests the speaker is overbearing, domineering ■ 'shrink' suggests the restrictive, claustrophobic nature of marriage ■ the comparison of the inner rings of an onion to a wedding ring suggests the constraining nature of marriage ■ the positioning of 'Lethal' in a line of its own suggests the dangerous nature of love ■ repetition and/or word choice of 'cling' suggests the possessive nature of love ■ 'knife' suggests a threatening, violent, dangerous aspect to love ■ the juxtaposition of 'fingers' and 'knife' suggests that something which should be gentle and loving (as in the caressing of the skin) has violent, destructive connotations.
40			Candidates can answer in bullet points in this final question, or write a number of linked statements. Marks for this question should be allocated following the guidelines given at the start of these Marking Instructions. See page 165.	10	Possible references include: ■ *Valentine* – several bizarre images to describe the negative power of love: 'blind you with tears like a lover', 'a wobbling photo of grief'; word choice such as 'fierce kiss', 'cling' ■ *Havisham* – imagery to describe speaker's distress: 'dark green pebbles for eyes'; word choice such as 'puce curses' to suggest distorted senses ■ *Originally* – imagery: 'anxiety stirred like a loose tooth' to convey niggling worry in her mind, 'tongue/shedding its skin like a snake' to describe the slow change in accent; word choice: 'skelf of shame' to suggest that shame causes minor discomfort ■ *Mrs Midas* – imagery: 'unwrapping each other, rapidly,/like presents' to convey the passion in their previous life, 'amber eyes/holding their pupils like flies' to suggest the horror of the dream; word choice: 'luteous' – very obscure word to describe the appearance of the cigarette ■ *Anne Hathaway* – series of images in opening lines to convey the whirlwind pleasure of their love, the series of comparisons with writing, drama; word choice: 'dozed' and 'dribbling' to describe the occupants of the 'other bed' ■ *War Photographer* – religious imagery in opening lines; word choice: 'prick/with tears' to suggest the inadequacy of the newspaper readers' response.

Text 3 – Poetry – *The Bargain* by Liz Lochhead

Question	Expected response	Max. mark	Additional guidance
41	2 marks may be awarded for detailed/insightful comment plus quotation/reference. 1 mark for more basic comment plus quotation/reference. 0 marks for quotation/reference alone. (Marks may be awarded 2+2, 2+1+1 or 1+1+1+1.)	4	Possible answers include: ■ 'queue' has connotations of delay, annoyance ■ 'blue haze of hot fat' suggests unhealthy, unpleasant, smothering, slightly dangerous ■ 'grit/our teeth' – wordplay suggests tension, irritation in the relationship ■ alliteration in 'grit … granules' suggests harsh, annoying ■ 'I keep/losing you and finding you' – double meaning: literal at the market, metaphorically suggests a troubled, on-off relationship ■ 'you thumb … I rub' suggests activities which, though similar, are separate ■ the two items ('manuals for/primary teachers' and 'dusty Chinese saucer') seem to vie with each other for uselessness, suggesting that the looking is mostly a displacement activity ■ 'till the gilt shows through' – image of getting to the reality of something + pun on 'guilt', suggesting her feelings ■ tone of 'Oh come on' suggests irritation, impatience ■ 'trap' suggests being tricked, forced ■ stallholder's comments seem to reflect on the couple's uneasiness, with mention of 'death' and 'doldrums', which could equally apply to the relationship.
42	2 marks may be awarded for detailed/insightful comment plus quotation/reference. 1 mark for more basic comment plus quotation/reference. 0 marks for quotation/reference alone. (Marks may be awarded 2+2, 2+1+1 or 1+1+1+1.)	4	Possible answers include: ■ 'packing up time' suggests something coming to an end; literally the stallholders are packing up, but the relationship seems to be also at that stage ■ 'the dark coming early' is both literal and metaphorical – a symbolic darkness falling on the relationship, with 'early' suggesting she thinks it is coming prematurely ■ 'beady bag' is a curiously vague and inelegant way to describe the bag, perhaps suggesting she feels foolish for buying it ■ 'maybe rosewood' suggests it may not be of any value ■ 'the inlaid butterfly' – a living creature depicted as inanimate, symbolic of the fading relationship ■ 'broken catch' symbolic of the broken relationship, whatever should hold it together ('the catch') is broken ■ 'waistcoat that needs a stitch' suggests something needing repair, as does the relationship ■ 'it just won't get' is pessimistically certain that no mending will happen ■ the rather enigmatic book title, *Enquire Within – Upon Everything*, suggests that solutions to all problems can be easily found – something she knows in her heart is not true.

Question			Expected response	Max. mark	Additional guidance
43			2 marks may be awarded for detailed/insightful comment plus quotation/reference. 1 mark for more basic comment plus quotation/reference. 0 marks for quotation/reference alone. (Marks may be awarded 1+1.)	2	Possible answers include: <ul><li>pessimistic: physical discomfort of the cold getting even worse suggests no improvement</li><li>pessimistic: the lack of communication is a reflection of the emptiness in the relationship and/or the fact that they are only too aware of the problems, no need or desire to discuss them</li><li>optimistic: 'I wish …' could be seen to have a positive tone, hoping that they might 'learn'</li><li>either: the strong rhyme at end ('say … away') could suggest a harmonious, tidy conclusion or a sense of finality, drawing a veil over matters.</li></ul>
44			Candidates can answer in bullet points in this final question, or write a number of linked statements. Marks for this question should be allocated following the guidelines given at the start of these Marking Instructions. See page 165.	10	Possible references include: <ul><li>*The Bargain* – friction – (implicit and explicit) between speaker and partner throughout: 'we're in love aren't we?', 'There doesn't seem to be a lot to say'; the projection of the disintegrating relationship onto the surroundings ('splintering city … wintry bridges')</li><li>*Last Supper* – friction in the relationship ('betrayal with a kiss') leading to the bitchy discussion of the break-up 'among friends', and the implied repetition: 'go hunting again'</li><li>*For My Grandmother Knitting* – tension between grandmother and her children over her knitting; they see it as unnecessary, when in fact it is her way of maintaining her usefulness</li><li>*My Rival's House* – tension between the speaker and her prospective mother-in-law due to her overprotectiveness of her son: 'this son she bore … never can escape', 'thinks she means me well', 'She won't/give up'</li><li>*Some Old Photographs* – tension between past and present</li><li>*View of Scotland/Love Poem* – some tension between speaker and mother in opening recollection.</li></ul>

Text 4 – Poetry – *Assisi* by Norman MacCaig

Question			Expected response	Max. mark	Additional guidance
45			2 marks may be awarded for detailed/insightful comment plus quotation/reference. 1 mark for more basic comment plus quotation/reference. 0 marks for quotation/reference alone. (Marks may be awarded 1+1.)	2	Possible answers include: <ul><li>the sibilance in 'sat, slumped' suggests lethargy, discomfort</li><li>the long vowel sounds in 'sat, slumped' suggest heaviness, tiredness</li><li>the onomatopoeic effect in 'slumped' to suggest heaviness, defeat, echoes of 'lump', 'dumped'</li><li>the alliteration in 'tiny twisted' draws attention to the unpleasantness, ugliness</li><li>the line break between 'which' and 'sawdust' creates a small dramatic pause before the horror of the description.</li></ul>
46			2 marks may be awarded for detailed/insightful comment plus quotation/reference. 1 mark for more basic comment plus quotation/reference. 0 marks for quotation/reference alone. (Marks may be awarded 2+2, 2+1+1 or 1+1+1+1.)	4	Possible answers include: <ul><li>juxtaposition of grand church ('three tiers') with St Francis' reputation ('brother/of the poor') and/or his simple lifestyle ('talker with birds')</li><li>sardonic observation that the dwarf has an 'advantage' over St Francis, but only that he is 'not ... dead yet'</li><li>'A priest explained ...' – what might seem at first to be praise for/approval of the priest is undermined by the realisation that the 'goodness/of God' is not evident in the 'suffering' of the dwarf</li><li>presenting himself as the detached observer with mock admiration for the priest's 'cleverness'</li><li>if 'I understood' is read with emphasis on 'I', it might suggest the tourists and/or the priest didn't understand.</li></ul>
47			2 marks may be awarded for detailed/insightful comment plus quotation/reference. 1 mark for more basic comment plus quotation/reference. 0 marks for quotation/reference alone. (Marks may be awarded 2+2, 2+1+1 or 1+1+1+1.)	4	Possible answers include: <ul><li>'ruined' in the sense that he is physically deformed, a distortion of a so-called normal human being:<ul><li>'eyes/wept pus' – not shedding tears in conventional way, but leaking infected fluid</li><li>ugly sound of word 'pus'</li><li>heavy sound of three stressed syllables</li><li>'back ... higher/than his head' – distortion of the normal</li></ul></li><li>a 'temple' in the sense of something with deep religious significance, often of immense beauty:<ul><li>despite all the unpleasant surface appearances, the dwarf is polite ('*Grazie*')</li><li>his voice is compared with that of a child (innocent) speaking to its mother (Madonna and child idea)</li><li>compared with a bird (nature, innocence) speaking to St Francis (icon of compassion, humility).</li></ul></li></ul>

Question			Expected response	Max. mark	Additional guidance
48			Candidates can answer in bullet points in this final question, or write a number of linked statements. Marks for this question should be allocated following the guidelines given at the start of these Marking Instructions. See page 165.	10	Possible references include: ■ *Assisi* – the tongue-in-cheek 'over whom/he had the advantage/of not being dead yet'; mockery of the tourists in 'clucking contentedly,/fluttered' ■ *Visiting hour* – the disembodied nostrils; the jokey confusion of 'here and up and down and there'; the vampire image reversed in 'not guzzling but giving' ■ *Aunt Julia* – the observation about boots: 'when she wore any'; the list beginning 'She was buckets …' ■ *Basking shark* – the parenthetical '(too often)' after 'once'; the description of the shark as a 'roomsized monster with a matchbox brain'; the unusual word 'shoggled' ■ *Sounds of the Day* – the light-hearted personification of 'a lapwing seeing us off the premises'; the child-like onomatopoeia of 'A snuffling puff …'.

Text 5 – Poetry – *Shores* by Sorley MacLean

Question			Expected response	Max. mark	Additional guidance
49			2 marks may be awarded for detailed/insightful comment plus quotation/reference. 1 mark for more basic comment plus quotation/reference. 0 marks for quotation/reference alone. (Marks may be awarded 2+2, 2+1+1 or 1+1+1+1.)	4	Possible answers include: ■ imagery: 'great white mouth … two hard jaws' personifies the bay as capable of devouring; the promontories as the powerful 'jaws' ready to snap shut ■ 'beside the sea/renewing love' suggests the healing power of the sea, able to renew something as powerful as love ■ 'the ocean was filling/Talisker bay forever' suggests eternal power of the ocean ■ 'Prishal bowed his stallion head' compares landscape feature to a powerful, graceful animal.
50			2 marks may be awarded for detailed/insightful comment plus quotation/reference. 1 mark for more basic comment plus quotation/reference. 0 marks for quotation/reference alone. (Marks may be awarded 1+1.)	2	Possible answers include: ■ 'I would stay there till doom' – i.e. until the end of time, a strong, if conventional, promise of fidelity ■ 'measuring sand, grain by grain' – an exaggerated notion of counting out an almost infinite number ■ 'I would wait there forever' – promising eternal devotion ■ 'the sea draining drop by drop' – another infinite task.

Question			Expected response	Max. mark	Additional guidance
51			2 marks may be awarded for detailed/insightful comment plus quotation/ reference. 1 mark for more basic comment plus quotation/ reference. 0 marks for quotation/ reference alone. (Marks may be awarded 2+2, 2+1+1 or 1+1+1+1.)	**4**	Possible answers include: ■ structural similarities with verses 1 and 2 ('And if I were ... I would ... I would') help round off the key idea of all-powerful love ■ repetition of 'shore' from verse 1 gives idea of preparing for conclusion and suggesting that any and every 'shore' would have the same effect ■ use of 'I' as opposed to 'we' suggests a narrowing of the focus ■ continues the idea of the power of nature, but combines elements from previous verses ('ocean and the sand, drop and grain') as if building to a climax ■ reinforces the idea of commitment ('synthesis of love for you') ■ concludes on a very personal desire to protect ('I would build the rampart wall').
52			Candidates can answer in bullet points in this final question, or write a number of linked statements. Marks for this question should be allocated following the guidelines given at the start of these Marking Instructions. See page 165.	**10**	Possible references include: ■ *Shores* – many references to natural features; suggests love is as powerful and enduring as these features and that he will protect the lover from any hostile natural forces ■ *Hallaig* – describes the mountains ('Cnoc an Ra'), the woods, and other natural features ('the Burn of Fearns') as background to observations about the effects of the passage of time in general and of the Clearances in particular ■ *Screapadal* – extensive references to landscape ('Carn Mor ... Creag Mheircil ... Raasay ... Maol Rubha ...') as context for exploration of the effects of the Clearances and of the presence of warships ■ *An Autumn Day* – reference to 'the stars of Africa,/ jewelled and beautiful' adds a certain poignancy to the horrific deaths being described.

Text 6 – Poetry – *The Thread* by Don Paterson

Question			Expected response	Max. mark	Additional guidance
53			2 marks may be awarded for detailed/insightful comment plus quotation/reference. 1 mark for more basic comment plus quotation/reference. 0 marks for quotation/reference alone. (Marks may be awarded 1+1.)	2	Possible answers include: <ul><li>'made his landing' – compares baby with something arriving, descending from the sky, depicting his birth as something exciting, mystical</li><li>'ploughed straight back into the earth' – compares baby with something disastrous, hinting at death, burial</li><li>'the thread of his one breath' compares his life to a single, fragile strand by which 'they' held on to him and rescued him; expresses his wonder, his gratitude.</li></ul>
54			2 marks may be awarded for detailed/insightful comment plus quotation/reference. 1 mark for more basic comment plus quotation/reference. 0 marks for quotation/reference alone. (Marks may be awarded 2+2, 2+1+1 or 1+1+1+1.)	4	Possible answers include: <ul><li>'I thank what higher will/brought us' – gratitude to a higher power (expressed in a rather vague way: 'what' seems to imply 'whatever – I don't really know or care')</li><li>'the great twin-engined swaying wingspan' – metaphor used to describe the appearance of him and his children arms out and linked (him as fuselage, children as wings/engines), suggests a feeling of joy, power within the family unit</li><li>'roaring down' – noisy, enjoying themselves thoroughly</li><li>out-revving/every engine in the universe' – exaggeration to convey his pride, relief, delight that the boy's lungs are healthy.</li></ul>
55			2 marks may be awarded for detailed/insightful comment plus quotation/reference. 1 mark for more basic comment plus quotation/reference. 0 marks for quotation/reference alone. (Marks may be awarded 2+2, 2+1+1 or 1+1+1+1.)	4	Possible answers include: <ul><li>continues image of the 'thread' (from title and line 3) as what holds life together, but now applied to whole family, not just Jamie</li><li>'all of us' emphasises the unity within the family</li><li>'tiny house' conveys the distance they are at the moment from home, but even so, the thread unifies them, holds them together</li><li>very personal 'us ... our ... son ... your' continues personal nature of the whole poem</li><li>image of the mother waving, despite her being only a 'white dot', is welcoming, warm, a very optimistic, uplifting way to conclude the poem.</li></ul>

Question			Expected response	Max. mark	Additional guidance
56			Candidates can answer in bullet points in this final question, or write a number of linked statements. Marks for this question should be allocated following the guidelines given at the start of these Marking Instructions. See page 165.	10	Possible references include: ■ *The Thread* – in sonnet form, with fixed/traditional structure and rhyme scheme; appropriately associated with expressions of love, tenderness, affection; could be seen to suggest idea of continuity in this poem ■ *Waking With Russell* – in sonnet form, not a standard type: sestet precedes octave; rhymes/off-rhymes ababab throughout; perhaps to reflect change in his life ■ *11.00: Baldovan* – couplets of half-rhyme; suitable for the rather strange, unnerving experiences being described in the poem ■ *Nil, Nil* – in three sections of unrhymed verse; typical line is 12 syllables, roughly iambic rhythm; last (short) section in italics to mark off as direct address to reader; appropriate for 'storytelling' style ■ *Two Trees* – two sections of rhymed iambic pentameter; suitable for old-fashioned, folk-tale type of narrative ■ *The Ferryman's Arms* – in two sections (pool room and ferry) of unrhymed verse; irregular line length and meter; could be seen to reflect the mysterious, enigmatic nature of the experience described in the poem.

C

Section 2 – Critical Essay – 20 marks

Supplementary marking grid

	Marks 20–19	Marks 18–16	Marks 15–13	Marks 12–10	Marks 9–6	Marks 5–0
Knowledge and understanding The critical essay demonstrates:	thorough knowledge and understanding of the text perceptive selection of textual evidence to support line of argument which is fluently structured and expressed perceptive focus on the demands of the question	secure knowledge and understanding of the text detailed textual evidence to support line of thought which is coherently structured and expressed secure focus on the demands of the question	clear knowledge and understanding of the text clear textual evidence to support line of thought which is clearly structured and expressed clear focus on the demands of the question	adequate knowledge and understanding of the text adequate textual evidence to support line of thought which is adequately structured and expressed adequate focus on the demands of the question	limited evidence of knowledge and understanding of the text limited textual evidence to support line of thought which is structured and expressed in a limited way limited focus on the demands of the question	very little knowledge and understanding of the text very little textual evidence to support line of thought which shows very little structure or clarity of expression very little focus on the demands of the question
Analysis The critical essay demonstrates:	perceptive analysis of the effect of features of language/filmic techniques	detailed analysis of the effect of features of language/filmic techniques	clear analysis of the effect of features of language/filmic techniques	adequate analysis of the effect of features of language/filmic techniques	limited analysis of the effect of features of language/filmic techniques	very little analysis of features of language/filmic techniques
Evaluation The critical essay demonstrates:	committed evaluative stance with respect to the text and the task	engaged evaluative stance with respect to the text and the task	clear evaluative stance with respect to the text and the task	adequate evidence of an evaluative stance with respect to the text and the task	limited evidence of an evaluative stance with respect to the text and the task	very little evidence of an evaluative stance with respect to the text and the task
Technical Accuracy The critical essay demonstrates:	few errors in spelling, grammar, sentence construction, punctuation and paragraphing the ability to be understood at first reading		clear evaluative stance with respect to the text and the task (—)	adequate focus on the demands of the question (—)	significant number of errors in spelling, grammar, sentence construction, punctuation and paragraphing which impedes understanding	

Acknowledgements

The Publishers would like to thank the following for permission to reproduce copyright material:

pp.3–4 The article 'The sooner zoos become extinct the better' by Janice Turner, from *The Times* © The Times/News Syndication, 4 June 2016.

pp.5–6 Text courtesy of PETA: www.peta.org.

pp.9, 40–41 and **70–71** extracts from *The Slab Boys* © 1982 John Byrne. *The Slab Boys* was first performed at the Traverse Theatre, Edinburgh, on 6 April 1978. All rights whatsoever in this play are strictly reserved and application for performance etc. should be made to the Author's agent: Casarotto Ramsay & Associates Limited, Waverley House, 7–12 Noel Street, London W1F 8GQ (rights@casarotto.co.uk). No performance may be given unless a licence has been obtained.

pp.10–11, 42 and **72** extracts from *The Cheviot, the Stag and the Black, Black Oil* by John McGrath. © John McGrath, 1981. Published by Bloomsbury Methuen Drama, an imprint of Bloomsbury Publishing Plc.

pp.12–13, 43–44 and 73–74 extracts from *Men Should Weep* © Ena Lamont Stewart, 1947. Reproduced by permission of Alan Brodie Representation Ltd (www.alanbrodie.com).

p.14 extract from 'The Red Door', **pp.44–45** extract from 'The Crater' and **pp.74–75** extract from 'The Painter' by Iain Crichton Smith, from *The Red Door: The Complete English Stories 1949–76*, published by Birlinn. Reproduced with permission of Birlinn Limited via PLSclear.

pp.15–16 extract from 'A Time To Keep', **p.46** extract from 'The Bright Spade' and **p.76** extract from 'The Eye Of The Hurricane' by George Mackay Brown, from *A Time To Keep*, published by Polygon. Reproduced with permission of Birlinn Limited via PLSclear.

pp.17, 47 and **77–78** extracts from *The Trick is to Keep Breathing* by Janice Galloway, published by Vintage, reprinted by permission of The Random House Group Limited. US & Canadian rights held by Dalkey Archive Press.

pp.18–19, 48–49 and **79** extracts from *Sunset Song* by Lewis Grassic Gibbon, published by Jarrold Publishing, 1932. Public domain.

pp.19–20, 50 and **80–81** extracts from *The Cone-Gatherers* by Robin Jenkins, published by Canongate Books Ltd.

pp.21–22 'A Poet's Welcome to His Love-Begotten Daughter', **pp.51–52** 'To a Mouse' and **pp.81–82** 'Tam o'Shanter' by Robert Burns. Public domain.

pp.22–23 'Mrs Midas' by Carol Ann Duffy from *World's Wife* (MacMillan, 1999); **p.52** 'Anne Hathaway' by Carol Ann Duffy from *World's Wife* (MacMillan, 1999); **p.83** 'Valentine' by Carol Ann Duffy from *Mean Time* (Anvil Press, 1993). Copyright © Carol Ann Duffy. Reproduced by permission of the author c/o Rogers, Coleridge & White Ltd., 20 Powis Mews, London W11 1JN.